THE TRUSTED ADVISOR SALES ENGINEER

By JOHN CARE

Table Of Contents

Acknowledgements

I must thank many people for their support, for their ideas, for their encouragement, and, of course, for their advice. Travelling back over 25 years to the original spark of curiosity about becoming a Trusted Advisor, I need to thank Ted Yarnell, who initially challenged me, and Mark Hoffman (co-founder of Sybase), who first uttered that fateful phrase in front of me. I owe a big shout-out to Steve Rubich, Ed Kietlinski, Howie Kurlender, Gary McKoy, and Donna Dudek, as well as Frank Fallon, Michael Shilling, Peter Gialo, and Bridget Piraino as part of that Sybase Financial Services team.

Since then, many learned individuals have (unwittingly at times) helped formulate the concept and given my abstract ideas some substantial weight. So thanks to Chris Daly, Wendell Meeks, Eric Popiel, Al Gurock, Andrew Travis, Victor Morvillo, John Chiavelli, Kevin Batson, David Griffin, Jack Fine, Brian Baillod, Nigel Stoodley, Christof Willems, Mark Carberry, Jim Wagstaff, Stephen Day, Rafique Ahmed, Mark Carberry, Kathy Eastwood and Bill Balnave for their contributions.

In addition, I have the folks who have intersected my personal and professional life. They would be Sid Amster, Marc Schnabolk, Paul Tinnerello, Andy & Gail Reiss, Rick & Suzanne Hauswald, Joe & Sharon Weiss, Nick Dorney and Tom King. They have each taught me something extraordinary about the power of Trust and Friendship.

Next, we have two people who were the modern catalyst for writing this book. They are Charles Green (a co-author of the Trusted

Advisor and Trusted Advisor Field Book) and Andrea Howe. Together they laid the foundation for the Trust Equation, which finally convinced me that there was something about a Trusted Advisor that we could measure.

Moving to my clients, thanks to Rob Engle, Richard Jackson, Lisa Larson, Sean Wedige, Jon Parkes, Orcun Terzel, Allan Young, David Siles, Scott Lillis, Dan Bognar, Peter Doolan, Rob Kaloustian, Mikel Steadman, Greg Cooper, Andy Spencer, Anuja Sharma, Marc Macaluso, and Scott Wood. Plus, a tremendous thank-you to multiple SEs from companies such as Cisco, HP, Oracle, Intel, Rackspace, SAS, Salesforce.com, Palo Alto Networks, Juniper, Veeam, Red Hat, Autodesk, Aveva, and Citrix, who all made valuable contributions.

Finally, a mention of my family. To my oldest daughter Amanda, the only person in my family who actually understands what an SE does, and to my son and lawyer Matthew, who will argue with me about absolutely anything. Thanks for their trust in me as a parent and for making me a proud father. Lastly, to my wife, companion, Mistress Of Dragons, and Master Trusted Advisor of over 40 years – Allison. Thanks for all the hours you let me disappear into my home office to "get some writing done." I would never have finished this book without your amazing love and encouragement.

John Care

Longboat Key, Florida

September 2022

Introduction

When Aron Bohlig and I released Mastering Technical Sales: The Sales Engineer's Handbook back in 2001; it was written and published out of frustration. Although there were hundreds of books about Sales Processes and Techniques, there was nothing out there solely for the Sales Engineer. Much has changed since then, and many more resources are available – although the major sales process vendors continue to neglect 30-35% of their potential audience.

Our profession has advanced over the last 20 years as well. To the uninitiated, a Sales Engineer (or Sales Consultant, Solutions Architect, or one of 50 other names) is the technical arm and conscience of the sales force. Traditionally, the salesperson finds a lead, builds a relationship and then introduces the Sales Engineer (SE) to explain, demonstrate, persuade, and show how their technology is uniquely suited to solve the customer's business problem. The customer is delighted, and the rep closes the deal. Transaction finished. Repeat as needed.

That has, thankfully, changed. Today the role of the SE has expanded way past being a "demo monkey." Instead, companies expect the SE to shoulder more of the burden of account development and business relationship. As a result, some SEs struggle to move past the technology, get down to business, and leverage their innate strengths to build lasting and fruitful client relationships. I wrote this book to ease that transition – and here is how it all started.

It was a dark and stormy morning in Manhattan. There was snow on the ground and fire in the air. I was sitting in the 32nd floor office of Ted Yarnell, the Area General Manager of Sybase's Financial Services Sales Division, along with three of my Sales Engineering management peers. Although we had just finished a phenomenally successful year in 1995, things were not looking so good for 1996. The Sybase growth engine was spluttering, our #1 competitor, Oracle, was getting its mojo back, and some questionable product decisions around the core database had weakened our market share.

A very senior executive had flown in from corporate and uttered the timeless words: *"You and your teams are going to have to get closer to our customers than ever before. They're going to have to trust you in order to trust that our technology can help them. So you need to become their Trusted Advisor. It's the only way we can survive."*

We looked at each other:

"How do we become a Trusted Advisor?"

The very senior executive remained silent. Ted's answer was both typically sales-like and empowering. *"You're smart people, and you'll figure it out. You'll know it when you see it."*

I went back to my office, stared out the window at the swirling snow, thought about "it" for several hours, and then called a staff meeting the next day. We were smart people, and we would figure it out. We did. We created a plan to get closer to our customers, promoted it to the sales people – with the full support of the district sales manager – and then violently executed it. The rest of the company survived three months before the down draft hit them; the Financial Services vertical survived fifteen months. Customers bought from us because they trusted us. When things went wrong, we fixed them. We gave them advice – even recommending competing products and partners at times.

Were we working with great salespeople? Absolutely! Did I have a talented team of Sales Engineers? No doubt about it! Did I have a fantastic resource in the ideas of my SE peers? You bet! Yet our plan to engage more often and positively promote our reliability, credibility, and creatively position 'the art of the possible' made all the difference.

In the intervening years, I have often wondered if there was a way to measure trust and if there was a repeatable process for a Sales Engineer to gain the trust of both the customer and the sales force. Whenever I heard the "Trusted Advisor" label, my mind returned to that day in Manhattan. Fast forward to 2011. I am sitting in the back of a large conference room in Las Vegas at one of my client's annual Sales Kick Off events. Another senior executive climbs on stage and proceeds to tell the technical audience that they need to become Trusted Advisors – without giving a shred of evidence or help as to why that would be a good thing. Finally, the VP of Sales Engineering turns to me and asks, *"Can you help us?"*

"I believe I can," was my brave reply. This guide of ideas, best practices, and processes will allow you to start your journey to The Trusted Advisor Sales Engineer. In the spirit of full disclosure, if you've been following me for a few years through the newsletter, blog, or have attended a workshop, you may recognize some of the material. The book is a collection of theory, practical experience (gathered from many people), and "how-to" ideas. Some of it I've covered before in a newsletter article, but this is certainly the first time it has been gathered and put into a logical structure. You are reading the revised 2022 paperback edition, reformatted[1] and slightly updated from the original 2016 eBook.

You'll also discover this is a very personal book, as much of it is written in the first-person ("I") rather than in abstract third-party prose. Trust and Advice are personal. Your client relationships are personal. Business is ultimately personal.

---

[1] Which is an amazing challenge and takes almost as much time as writing.

How To Use The Book

There are three main sections in this book.

Section 1 – The Theory And The Process. It deals with defining the overall concept of the Trusted Advisor Sales Engineer, measuring the degree of trust in a relationship, and then the difficulty of even starting the process.

Section 2 – Putting It Into Practice. It looks at the practical issues of how an SE can introduce trust and best practices into customer and salesperson relationships.

Section 3 – Getting There From Here. It provides more of an organizational overview of how an individual SE or a small SE team can plan for the cultural and corporate changes necessary to make trust a behavior and a habit rather than "the next new thing."

The best way to read the book is to take it chapter-by-chapter and section by section. Just as there is no real shortcut to gaining someone's trust, there is no real shortcut to reading the book. It is essential that you have defined (at least in your mind) what a Trusted Advisor means to you, what it means to your customers, and what it means to your company, before you start trying to act like one. In fact, after running hundreds of sessions with my clients, I've discovered that even defining it mentally doesn't help that much. It may be old-fashioned, but you must **write it down** and share it with others. Trusted Advisor is indeed one of those "*I'll know it when I see it*" type of concept – one that results in twenty people in a class having thirty different definitions.

You will have to put some work into this book to get the most out of it. There are many exercises, worksheets, and thought experiments for you to try. In many of the chapters, there are case studies. Ask yourself what you would do in a similar situation. Then write it down. There are also many exercises and worksheets in the book or referenced on the website (www.masteringtechnicalsales.com/tabook).

At the end of most of the chapters in Section 2, there is a Skill Building section. These skills apply whether you have been an SE for two months, two years, or 20 years – practice them! If you are an old-hand experienced SE, you have had plenty of time to build bad habits. Take a fresh look at what you are doing and how you are doing it. Even if you decide that the measurement piece is not for you, you can still find many tips, techniques, and ideas to help you on the path to becoming, or remaining, a Trusted Advisor.

You may also note that throughout the book, in keeping with my Trans-Atlantic background, I randomly flip-flop between the US and UK versions of words such as colour / color and behaviour / behavior. You can't please all the people all the time – please ignore the inconsistency and look for the meaning behind the words instead! Trust me on that.

Any book references will usually link back to the US Amazon.com site. However, the majority of books I reference are available in multiple languages.

Please enjoy the read – and let's get started!

Bottom Line Up Front: What's In It For You?

I n the spirit of much of the advice within Mastering Technical Sales, I'll start with the Grand Finale. What is the impact of running a serious and focused Trusted Advisor (T/A) program on the Sales and Sales Engineering organizations? Those benefits may seem intuitively obvious. How could better client relationships hurt you in any way? Shouldn't you expect greater client engagement, improved access to the decision-makers, more references, and a host of other amazing results? Well, yes you should – except the Trusted Advisor route is not an easy path to travel down. It requires significant commitment, and ultimately you have to **prove** it works.

My client is a mid-size software company struggling with name recognition and brand awareness. They had robust and capable sales and sales engineer operations teams who could measure almost anything related to the customer buying process in extraordinary detail. Metrics were not going to be a problem, and there was commitment from the SVPs of Sales and Sales Engineering and active support from VPs of Marketing, Services, and Customer Support. Many of the metrics were definitely sales and revenue focused – but if you believe in a *"rising tide lifts all boats"* philosophy, happier clients, larger deals, fewer discounts, and ultimately less useless work have tremendous benefits to an SE organization. Plus, as many a VP of Sales has reminded me over the past 30 years, it is indeed that bottom line that generates paychecks, stock options, club trips, and all the other creature comforts of SE life.

We ran our Trusted Advisor program just for the Central Region in the US (for those outside the US, think of that as the states that don't touch the Atlantic or the Pacific Ocean). That left the East, West, and Federal regions as a baseline for the status quo. The program was supposed to run for a year, with regular quarterly assessments. After eleven months, the operations team presented this one slide to executive leadership. They concluded the experiment, called it an outright success and rolled out the program to the rest of the world.

The Numbers Say

53%	Reduction in RFPs from Strategic Accounts
142%	Increase in Corporate Visits
44%	Increase Reference–ability (NPS–linked)
3%	Reduction in Discount
19%	Increase in Deal Size
40%	Better Growth Than Other Districts
100%	Retention Rate for Key SE Performers
22%	Reduction in Salesrep Turnover

Figure 1: Fantastic Trusted Advisor Program Metrics

Those are undoubtedly great numbers, so let's look at each in more detail to understand their logic and cause.

RFP Reduction

On an annualized basis, the number of RFPs received from their Strategic Accounts was cut in half. Strategic Accounts are a combination of the top two customer tiers comprising Global/National accounts and Top 100 regional accounts. The central part of the reduction was because these Strategic Accounts offered my client the business without going through the complex and time-consuming RFP process. A minor part was due to accounts NOT feeling obliged to send an RFP to my customer for business they couldn't possibly win. This situation leads to a different

THE TRUSTED ADVISOR SALES ENGINEER

question of why they even bothered to respond in the first place – but that was an internal trust issue between sales and sales engineering. The critical outcome is that they won some deals they wouldn't have won before and accelerated those deals they would have won anyway. In addition, the SE team could spend more time focusing on higher-value parts of the sales process. Everyone wins.

Corporate Visits

My client had also noted that inducing a corporate visit during a major sales opportunity was a significant leading indicator of success. Given that US corporate headquarters was on the west coast, it certainly meant that the customer had to make a time and money commitment to travel, and 91% of corporate visits foreshadowed a deal in that or the following quarter. Over the twelve months of the T/A program, the number of visits more than doubled, and the close rate remained in the low 90s. By building a better relationship with their clients, the salesforce could gain the commitment to visit the corporate headquarters, meet with company executives, and learn more about strategy.

References (NPS score)

Net Promoter Score[2] measures customer satisfaction and how likely your clients will recommend you to another potential client. As such, a high NPS aids the sales cycle as you have additional voices inside your customer base, helping you to sell. Over twelve months, the regional NPS score (which measured sales, presales, and professional services) increased by 44%, sufficient to move the team directly into the promoter segment and out of the detractor segment. From the SE viewpoint, this helped considerably with reducing the amount of work required to "lock" reference architectures into place and assisted in eliminating a few Proof Of Concepts that were sold by references instead.

---

[2] http://www.netpromoter.com/Home

Reduction In Discount

The overall discount rate for each major transaction (directly handled by the field-facing team) was reduced by 3.2%. This was even more impressive as the discount rate in other regions marginally increased. The cause and effect are still under investigation, but the salespeople reported less "friction in the deal," which resulted in fewer last-minute customer demands and concessions. Everyone paid on revenue (and even more so on operating profit) benefited from this outcome. Considering that the average deal size increased significantly (see next item), which would typically lead to an increase in the discount rate, this effect was even more notable.

Increase In Deal Size

Overall transaction size, measured as ASP(Average Selling Price) or YRR(Yearly Recurring Revenue) – increased by 19.5% over the prior year. There were no mitigating circumstances, such as price rises or new modules, so the increase was directly attributed to the T/A program. All aspects of the transaction increased in terms of cross-selling/up-selling, educational services, professional services, and consulting.

> **NOTE – Just to put those last two points in perspective, <u>the company received 22.7% more revenue for the same amount of work</u>.**

Overall Growth Rate

The Central Region outperformed all other regions by just over 40% in license and subscription growth. That growth was fueled by the deal size/discount rate changes, the RFP win rate increase, and simply competing in and winning more deals. The T /A program directly impacted each of these factors. (Given the size of each region, they judged that personnel turnover and skill sets remained relatively constant and had no more impact on the results). The growth was also relatively uniform across the region, so it was not disrupted by several massive transactions or just 20% of the salespeople exceeding quota.

Retention Rate For Key SE Performers

Over the past two years, the company experienced a 13% attrition rate for key SE performers (termed by Human Resources as "regrettable resignations"). However, during the initial T/A program and the following year – not a single SE left the company. This promoted stability, teamwork, increased bonuses, commissions, and stock price, which was certainly another factor in overall performance. The company estimated this saved them USD 150,000 in fully burdened costs for every SE that would have left. Plus, an estimated USD 3,000,000 hit to the pipeline.

Sales Representative Turnover

The company's business model was to hire a mix of experienced and junior salespeople and plan to lose a certain percentage every year to attrition or internal movement. The prior year's attrition rate was 35%. During the T/A program, it decreased to 12% - more salespeople were reaching quota and making extremely good money. The company estimated this saved them USD 112,000 in fully burdened costs for each salesperson retained and an additional USD 300,000 in opportunity costs per open territory.

Other Miscellaneous Items

These items were not directly measured but were reported anecdotally by multiple SEs and salespeople.

1. *Decrease In Active Deal Time.* The sales operations team believed deal velocity increased by about four days. Because of the difficulty in determining exactly when a deal went "live," it is not an accurate number but certainly shows a trend.

2. *Better Executive Access.* The sales teams reported that it was easier to get repeat meetings at the CIO and CIO-1 levels than before. They estimated average wait time decreased by about a week.

3. *Demo Reductions*. The number of formal SE-led demonstrations and presentations decreased from an estimated 4.2 per deal to just over 3. That caused a decrease in time spent per SE on demo preparation and demo presentation.

4. *Cross-Region Benefits*. Other regions gained an indeterminate benefit by utilizing the increased NPS and reference capability of the Central Region.

5. *Conflict*. Overall SE-Rep conflict (defined as when escalation occurs) rose by an estimate of 33% in the first four months – mainly around disagreements on the amount of discovery. The numbers declined to the initial steady state around months 6-7. They decreased by the end of the 11-month test period.

The Bottom Line

There is clearly both a soft and a hard economic benefit to running a T/A program in terms of revenue, margin, employee compensation, and general employee engagement and satisfaction.

So .. how can you do this?

Section 1: The Theory And The Process

"The Best Way To Find Out If You Can Trust Somebody Is To Trust Them"

- Ernest Hemingway

I f you are really in a hurry to get to the more practical aspects of being a Trusted Advisor Sales Engineer, you can read the first three chapters in Section 1 and then skip onto Section 2.

Since we'll use the phrase Trusted Advisor in the remainder of the book, I'll start using the abbreviation "T/A" to simplify things. That may well be the only simple thing in the following few chapters. Think of this as the more theoretical and cerebral part of the book, although I will put forward a mechanism you can develop to measure trust and assign it a number. Once you put a number on it, even as an approximation, it becomes easier to adapt your behavior to increase the score.

As SEs, we love to measure things and to get clearly defined success criteria, so that will be our end goal for the section. And since you will be building the score sheet and creating the scale, you only have yourselves to blame if it is still too fuzzy and imprecise. We will examine the five factors or attributes that go into the Trust score, how to create a scoring system or rubric, and then some more profound concepts around trust and advice. You'll also see customer data about the T/A and learn what your customers expect and value the most.

Then we'll finish with how to utilize the built-in advantages that SEs have over their sales counterparts (a secret weapon we don't use as much as we should) and ultimately look at the salesperson's initial view on implementing a T/A program.

Chapter 1: Defining A Trusted Advisor Sales Engineer

The most essential part of the definition is that the T/A label is NOT one that you can give yourself, nor is it one that the company can put on your business card. I only mention this because I've seen over a dozen companies allow and actively encourage their employees to use that title. Being a T/A is a label, or characteristic your customers apply to you. That is an important point, as the core of a T/A means looking at everything from your customer's viewpoint.

We can start by breaking the words apart. First, we have the "**Trust.**" What actually makes a customer trust you? It is much more than your technical knowledge and capabilities, as those are the basic table stakes that customers expect of any SE. For an SE, it is a combination of honoring your commitments, speaking the truth, and acting in the customer's best interests – even if that may occasionally conflict with the best interests of your own company.

Now we move on to "**Advice.**" We have all been in a situation when we have given people personal or professional advice, and they have ignored us. Your customers must be willing to listen to you before you can provide advice. What makes them ready to listen to you? Trust plus curiosity and experience.

When I ask a workshop with 20 SEs in it for their definitions of a T/A, I can get 30 or more answers in return. They all circle the same idea but approach it in different ways. It is a classic *"I'll know it when I see it"* concept. So, let's try to make all that a little more concrete with a few exercises for you to work through. Grab an old-fashioned (but highly functional) pen or open a document on your device.

Mini-Exercise #1.1: The Positive Attributes of A Trusted Advisor

Take about 2-3 minutes and write down as many words or phrases you associate with T/A – without using the words Trust or Advice. Capture some words that may be relatively generic and some that are more SE-specific towards the role. You will probably have used some phrases like:

Honest	Believable	Transparent
Straight Forward	Does The Right Thing	Reliable
Has Tough Conversations	Respect	Skilled
Professional	Open Minded	Knowledgeable
Listens	Valued	Keeps Confidences
Competent	Problem Solver	Great Attitude

Table 1.1 Sample Positive Attributes

[handwritten: Communicator, Curious, Seek to understand, Customer focused, Delivers/Follow through, Sure/confident of product knowledge]

Mini-Exercise #1.2: The Negative Attributes Of The Anti-Trusted Advisor

Now move to the other extreme and think about someone who is not a Trusted Advisor – the proverbial second-hand car or snake-oil salesman. Go through the same exercise and take 2-3 minutes to list words or phrases that describe non-T/A behavior. This is a more straightforward list to generate – just don't write down any names of people you have worked with in the past!

[handwritten: T/A.]

You will probably have used some phrases like:

Dishonest	Unreliable	Just Talks
Does Not Listen	Own Agenda	Me, Me and Me
Pushy	Arrogant	All Promises
Self-Serving	Transactional	Lone Wolf
Condescending	Unethical	Not Accountable

Table 1.2 Sample Negative Attributes

We've now bracketed the extremes by examining the positive and negative attributes that we associate with the position or behavior of a T/A. Keep that list around for a few more chapters, as we'll return to this concept. It's now time to make it a little more personal.

Mini-Exercise #1.3: Your Personal Examples

Now think of one or more people in your personal or professional life who you consider to be your Trusted Advisors. This is another writing exercise. Write down:

a. The person's name (try not to use your current manager or a parent — that's far too easy for most of us!).
b. What their particular area of expertise may be.
c. Some specific examples of actions/behaviors they have performed that cause you to think of them as your personal T/A.

Some of my examples:

1. I've known Sid Amster since 1988 when I first met him at Oracle. We quickly developed a rapport and stayed in touch over the years. Sid has always made time to help me, guided me through a career crisis, and provided the impetus to write an article for CIO magazine about hiring practices that initially got me noticed in the "author community." He is now a major figure in the Philadelphia VC arena, yet he still takes time to grab lunch or dinner, suggests contacts, and gives me new ideas.

2. Peter has been a friend of mine since 2004. That's Peter Cohan — author of "Great Demo!³" He was instrumental in guiding me when I transitioned into running my company as a full-time business many years ago. He advised, critiqued my training materials, and even threw me a few leads. That's strange — technically, we market to the same customers. Yet the market is so large, we both have a different focus, and we both love the Sales Engineer profession

---

³ http://www.secondderivative.com/ Great Demo!

that he was willing to help me. In the intervening years, I'd like to think I've repaid some of that initial kindness, but he certainly stopped me from making a considerable number of mistakes.

3. Margaret at my local Staples Office Supplies store. Over the past few years, she has saved me a small fortune on printer supplies and binders by pointing out coupons, multi-packs, and special offers—less money for Staples, more for me. Except last year, I bought a new laptop, printer, and home phone system at Staples instead of Best Buy. Trust! Doing the right thing for the customer almost invariably results in a longer-term financial return for you.

What's the point of this exercise? Take a mental snapshot of your feelings about that personal T/A you just listed. The way that you feel about them is the way that you want your customers, partners, and colleagues to think of you. It's not even a typical "warm and fuzzy" feeling; it is more a feeling of certainty, 100% trust, and confidence. That is your mental and emotional beacon for the rest of the book!

In the next chapter, we'll examine the five factors that broadly comprise Trust and how to measure them. But, before we do that – try a mini exercise in the form of three preliminary questions.

Mini-Exercise #1.4: Trust And Advice

Question #1: What can you do to show one of your customers that you are acting in their best interest? (It does not have to involve saving money). *Soloution (customised to their process, company or Devision.*

Question #2: Think about a recent situation when you provided (good) advice that was ignored. Why did that happen? (The other person was a complete idiot is NOT the answer you should be looking for!) *Resistant to Change or to Apply Best practices.*

Question #3: Think about a recent situation when you provided (good) advice – and it was taken. Why did that happen?

Pain of Change was < Change - offer a solution at time of need

Mini-Exercise #1.5: Your First Definition

Here are some guidelines.

1. Try for 140 characters or less – make it an old-style (2016!) tweet.
2. Avoid using "Trust" or "Advice" in the definition.
3. If you like your definition, tweet/send it to me. (@PresalesMTS [4] using the hashtag *#tabook*)
4. Don't stop at a single definition.

Give it a try!

In Summary

The summary is that it is time to make your first attempt at a definition of a Trusted Advisor. This is your beta version, and you'll have many opportunities to refine it as you progress through the book. Every time you think of a better word or phrase or overall definition, write it down.

5/23 @ NOON 11 am .

Chapter 2: How Do We Measure Trust?

Now, I'll introduce you to a methodology that can give you a numerical measure of Trust. This is the longest chapter and sets the basis for everything else in the book. You should read the chapter several times to fully grasp the concepts and deeper meaning of the Trust factors. Once more, please trust me on this!

A good starting point is to build on the groundbreaking work of Charles Green, David Maister, and Robert Galford in their book, The Trusted Advisor[5]. I'd recommend it as required background reading; it is undoubtedly the basis and inspiration for this chapter. Charles also puts out a semi-weekly newsletter/blog worth reading[6].

They defined trust as measured by the four factors of Credibility, Reliability, Intimacy, and Self-Orientation. We will describe these later in the chapter as to how they relate to an SE. With permission, I adapted their equation and added a "**P**" at the end to account for Positivity to get an interesting mnemonic – **CRISP**.

$$ T = \left[\frac{C+R+I}{S} \right] P $$

Figure 2.1: The Updated Trust Equation

---

[5] http://www.amazon.com/Trusted-Advisor-David-H-Maister/dp/0743212347/
[6] http://trustedadvisor.com/

Mathematically we would like T to be as high as possible, meaning that **Credibility**, **Reliability,** and **Intimacy** at the top of the equation are POSITIVE factors (we want big numbers). On the other hand**, Self-Orientation** is a NEGATIVE factor as it is on the bottom of the equation, so we want a low number for that. This is about as complicated as the math gets, so don't worry. **Positivity** is an overall multiplier that can shift the raw Trust score up or down a little.

Scoring The Factors – An Explanation

We will develop a scoring scale, or rubric, for each factor – but we will look at it in two ways. The first is based on the actions you take, the things you do, your manner of building relations etc. The second is based on how the customer sees and interacts with you. You will discover that it does not matter too much how you initially score yourself; what's more important is how the customer "scores" you in their behaviors with you.

There is a sample blank score sheet at the end of this chapter and templates for the score sheet on the website. The scoring ranges from **1** to **5**. Where **1** is a low score in the factor, and **5** is the highest score.

It would help to decide what "normal, acceptable business behavior" is as an organization or an individual. Many clients adopt a **3** as the normal/average, with **5** being a stretch goal for world-class and **1** being about every poor behavior you can think of that would sabotage a relationship. That means that most individual factor scores would be in the **2-4** range because if you get a **1** for **C, R, or I** and/or a **5** for **S,** you shouldn't be in sales and will probably get fired. Note that Positivity (P) has a different scale, which we will deal with later in the chapter.

TIP – I'd strongly recommend that you only deal with integers, except for Positivity. It may upset some of the more data-driven SEs, but it makes the math easier to do in your head!

Characteristic	High (Good) Score	Low (Bad) Score
C Credibility	5	1
R Reliability	5	1
I Intimacy	5	1
S Self-Orientation	1	5
P Positivity	1.33	0.5

Table 2.1: Possible Ranges Of Scores For The Five CRISP Factors

C-Credibility.

The great thing about being an SE is that you automatically bring some credibility to the sales situations. When you and the salesperson are together, you are considered more credible because you are not "in sales." You can further break this down by evaluating if you are believable at the time you speak/act and if you are ultimately proved "right"?

One of the biggest "C" traps is the feeling that you must prove your value every minute you are in a meeting. Sometimes the best credibility comes from listening extremely hard and then speaking. The counterpoint to high credibility might be that you are viewed as someone who loves to hear themselves talk (even though what you say might be accurate and valuable). From a customer viewpoint, a quite simple two-part definition of SE Credibility is *"Does the customer believe what I say, and do they see the value in what I say?"* Although Competency is a close cousin of Credibility – they are not the same. You can be competent (knowledge + experience) but not always credible. If you have ever given someone else great advice, which they ignore because they don't believe you, you have experienced that gap between those two words.

Credibility is the easiest of the five factors for an SE to achieve and even over-achieve. As techies, we tend to pride ourselves on our technical ability to be accurate, precise, and knowledgeable. That pride shows in being able to answer as many questions as we possibly can about our product or service, knowing the details of every bullet point in Product Marketing's "Grand Tour" slide deck, and being able to navigate to almost any menu option during a demo, whilst simultaneously reciting product specifications in both imperial and metric units.

A modest amount of customer Credibility does not take a significant amount of time to gain, as one or two good meetings can give you a solid score. The downside is that once an SE loses their credibility with a customer, it can be exceedingly difficult to regain it. Giving vague or misleading answers to a question or being factually incorrect are classic examples.

Remember that being credible and knowledgeable ("smart") just for its own sake won't do it. If you are not providing value with credibility (i.e. technical or business insight), then you are dealing with technical "speed and feeds." Very few customers will care about that kind of data if it is already on your website. However, unlike your sales counterpart, you will sometimes deal with customer personnel who genuinely care about the numbers and the speed and feeds metrics. Feature-function conversations get a bad name in the sales process. Still, sometimes the SE is presenting to a bunch of techies in the basement conference room (the one with the noisy heating unit and no windows) and needs to know the product specifications. Not every SE presentation is Steve Jobs style simplicity with aesthetic beauty.

Precision and accuracy are easy enough habits for the SE to embrace, but that needs to partner with the personality that interprets and drives that knowledge across to the customer. That is precisely the reason why we have dual self and customer scoring!

Six Ways To Gain Credibility

1. **Tell The Truth**. Always. Plus, you get the benefit of never having to remember what you said!

2. **Be Considerate With That Truth.** Unfortunately, younger SEs can sometimes be too blunt – directly saying, *"that is never going to work!"* to your client may not be the best approach.

3. **Use *I Don't Know* Wisely**. If you do not know the answer to a question, say so, and then promise to get it for the customer. Do not guess! You can only do this a few times in a meeting – excessive "don't knows" shows that someone is in the wrong meeting. Sometimes it's you; sometimes, it is the customer.

4. **Show Passion**. Show passion and enthusiasm for your product/solution/services and for helping the customer. Then, relax and take a deep breath so you do not speak too quickly from an adrenaline high.

5. **Utilize Your Credentials**. It's OK to cite your credentials, but don't overdo it and do make it relevant. So yes – you can put CISSP, ITIL, or vExpert on your business card and eSignature, but just use one. A raft of acronyms after your name is excessive. (Note: "MBA" won't make much difference in most countries.[7]) Also, be sensitive to cultures – someone else should cite your credentials in many parts of the world than use the US testosterone "in-your-face" approach.

6. **Do The Research**. Know as much as feasible about the company, its issues, and the people you meet. Just saying, *"I read that article in the Straits Times yesterday,"* can really help – as long as you actually did read it!

And Now The First Scorecard

To get you started for Credibility, I've supplied a few sample attributes and behaviors (Table 2.2) collected from classes over the past years to prime the pump. These are the client's own words and grammar. You must create your scorecard as that is the only way to get buy-in from others that reflects your corporate values and culture. Many teams use

---

[7] But it does in India, Germany and some other countries.

the "always / almost always / sometimes / rarely / never" scale to assist them in scoring, while others go for distinct behaviors.

	Trust Factor	CREDIBILITY
Score	Your Actions	Customer Actions
1	Poor appearance. Bad jokes. Misses Meetings. Unprepared. Dishonest. Goes way off script. BS's customer Screws up deal. All "No"	Complains to your manager or rep. Refuses to work with you. Snubs or yells at you. Totally disinterested. Reputation Killer. Abruptly ends meeting. Highly negative body language Questions everything with skepticism.
2	Lack of required tech skills. Low value and minimal impact. Rigid in planning. False/outdated info. Last minute preparation. Unorganized.	Asks for other "resources" instead of you. Always checking and confirming. Looks for reasons not to meet you. Cuts meetings short Disengaged. May be constantly checking email or phone. "On mute" for phone calls.
3	Do what is expected – and no more. Standard demo – no customer connection. Just-in-time planning/prep Answers standard questions with just enough info. A little scripted. Minimal value added.	Neither positive nor negative. Rep retains all responsibility for call. Hopes/expects more from you. Mostly engaged – good eye contact Allows follow-up when pressed
4	Adapts to situations. Balances Y/N. Adds (+) customer content. Gets 'nuggets' of info for rep from customer. Looks at alternatives. Shares customer stories. Expands expertise.	Puts you up front more often. Confident. Let's you work independently at times. Sometimes defers to you. Customer likes/asks for you. Engaged – positive body language Wants follow-up Recommends to others in his org
5	Comprehensive messaging. Addresses business pain. Client praise. Client excited. Teaches. Expands deal. Critical asset. Always 100% ready and prepared. IS THE EXPERT	Looks forward to meeting. Always available. Praise to management. Confident. Let's you be highly independent. Recommends to others in his company and outside the company. Totally engaged (on edge of seat) Asks questions non-product related.

Table 2.2: Sample Worksheet For Credibility

R-Reliability

Years ago, as a trainee Chemical Engineer, I went to a management class in England and was taught about a philosophy named **DAYS – Do As You Say**. That acronym has stayed with me ever since. If you are serious about becoming a T/A, it is not too hard for you to live up to your commitments and honour your word. This habit has a few far-reaching implications. First, you need to establish control of your time (calendar) and your inbox, as it is far more likely that lack of time, rather than lack of desire or talent, will hurt your reliability. Second, you need to be realistic and not always follow the SE instinct of automatically pleasing the customer or the salesperson.

What proves difficult is when other people in your organization impact the reliability measure. You can promise an answer in 24 hours, yet if Product Management does not get back to you, you are stranded. That is where realism and calendar control apply. My general rule was that unless someone had exhibited extreme reliability to me, I would assume their response would always take 50% longer. I would also assume that customer and internal issues would erode the big block of time I had reserved for myself tomorrow, so I would only have 50% of that available. Of course, that is a pessimistic view, but I feel that is life in the corporate world, plus it gives you a built-in opportunity to deliver ahead of time.

After Credibility, Reliability is another relatively easy factor for an SE to achieve a good score. Unlike Credibility, which can be established after just a few interactions, Reliability needs a more extended period, or at least more opportunities, so that you can demonstrate a pattern of good behavior. For example, two or three instances of delivering on or slightly ahead of time won't make you a "5" in Reliability. Still, they can set a foundation for the customer to trust in what you say you will accomplish. However, as we shall see, Reliability has greater depth than simply beating timeframes.

Six Ways To Gain Reliability

1. **Aim For Frequency**. Rather than meeting one massive commitment, subdivide it into a dozen smaller ones you can target and then exceed.

2. **Set A Structure**. Provide structure around everything. That means items such as agendas, goals, and promises.

3. **Double Confirm**. Write items down and then communicate them promptly to the client and the rest of the sales team. Then, when someone meets with you and reconfirms a few hours later that they have the task in hand and will get back to you by Thursday, doesn't that make you feel better? (Cultural note: writing everything down as a commitment can be a very western approach and may offend some other nationalities who consider their word their bond.) Verbally reconfirming what you have heard and then paraphrasing it for clarity seems to be a valued skill worldwide.

4. **Anticipate.** Reliability at its best isn't just doing what you say; it is also about anticipating what the customer may need and preparing for that eventuality.

5. **Set Homework**. Send your client pre-work and even homework. They'll appreciate the opportunity to be fully prepared and briefed. Whether they read the material is another issue.

6. **Be Personal**. Don't forget the personal side of things. Be emotionally consistent and professionally levelheaded. Note that this does not mean emotionally distanced and detached, but that you shouldn't be doom-and-gloom one day and rainbows and puppy dog happy the next.

Now complete a second scorecard for Reliability. Again, use the same criteria as you did for Credibility regarding what is "average" or "acceptable business behaviour."

I-Intimacy

Intimacy measures how well you know and understand the customer, personally and professionally. It does not necessarily mean that you know the name of their partner, children, and favorite coffee drink (although that may help), but that you understand their personal wins and feelings about any particular situation/sale. Essentially, it is all about putting yourself in the customer's shoes[8]. The intimacy also extends to the business issues, as (to foreshadow the next chapter) the #1 thing most mid to senior-level executives expect from a vendor's sales engineering organization is someone who understands their business.

Looking at Intimacy another way is that it teaches you how to communicate with the individual. Some people, and generations, prefer different forms of communication (email, text, face-to-face) and different mechanisms (fast, direct, data-driven). Your job as an SE is to adapt to your customer. We'll look at that area in much more detail in Chapter 20 – The Current State.

Based on our survey data from workshops, Intimacy is the weakest of the five factors for an SE in terms of their actual scores and rankings and how comfortable they are in discussing it. The job requires us to deal with hardware and software and processes and best practices, but the people who use them? That is a different story. Of course, that is also a gross generalization, but nonetheless, the data backs up the fact that most SEs will struggle with Intimacy compared to the other factors.

You can learn a lot more about me by reading this book, as many of the case studies revolve around the various successes and failures I have experienced over the years. Note that I share failures as well as successes. You can learn from them as I have, and there is a degree of rapport to build up by freely admitting my many imperfections. The level and type of information a customer shares with you can provide a clear estimate of the intimacy level.

---

[8] Showing empathy by looking at a situation from a different point of view; as if one were the other person

Six Ways To Gain Intimacy

1. **Apply The Personal To The Business**. We all have friends and relationships that we have built over the years. Look at how they have developed, your conversations, and the use of common interests.

2. **Ask Your Sales Partner**. It's a rare salesperson who will turn down the opportunity to teach an SE about relationship building and rapport. That has been one of my best learning sources.

3. **Use Food**. A meeting over breakfast or lunch, or even a cup of tea, can go a long way to building up some intimacy. There is more on this in Chapter 17 – the Social Sales Engineer.

4. **Be Brave**. It is not that scary. Quite often, all you must do is share something with your customer. Sports, children, and hobbies are good starters. Pets are often amazing. I used a photo of Yardley, my Golden Retriever[9], in several of my classes to good effect.

5. **Research** - without stalking your customer. You can sometimes find something in their background about schools, colleges, or organizations that can help you start the conversation.

6. **Practice** in a harmless situation. Next sports event, standing in line at a grocery store or a coffee shop, get your head out of the smartphone and start a conversation with a real person. (Great advice for our millennial children!)

Now complete the third scorecard for Intimacy. Use the same criteria as you did for the other sheets regarding "average" or "acceptable business behaviour." Pay special attention to contrasting your expected behaviours against the customers. This factor is frequently the one with the most variance between the columns.

---

[9] Who sadly woofed her last in 2018 but stays with me in my heart

S-Sense Of Self-Orientation

As S is in the equation's denominator (bottom), a low score is good, and a high score is terrible. This measures how much you think about yourself and your company versus the customer's needs. When you find yourself selling instead of solving, thinking of quota instead of discovery questions, or transactions instead of long-term strategy – then that is a high (and therefore a bad) S. This is the most problematic characteristic for an SE to adopt in a sales-driven culture given the pressures to help sales in *hitting the number* every month or every quarter. Mostly this will be external pressure from sales and your company rather than internal pressure from your heart or head. However, compared to your sales counterpart, you are ahead of them on this factor.

CASE STUDY: IT'S NOT WHAT YOU SAY BUT WHAT YOU DO...

"I'm a first-year associate at a prestigious management consulting company in the UK. Not a day goes by without someone higher up the chain of command reminding us that *"the customer comes first."* We are told, *"Do the right thing for the customer."* Yet not a week goes by without seeing several instances of those same senior managers flogging (Brit. slang for selling) unneeded services to our witless clients who trust us to keep them out of trouble. It's depressing and the major reason we have over 60% turnover within 18 months."

--- Simon, 1st Year Associate – Manchester, England.

Being Right Or Doing The Right Thing

SEs are rarely accused of being greedy or just being in it for the money (a.k.a. coin-operated), so their form of Self is usually a little more subtle. However, many issues around a poor S can come from having the good intentions of being the best SE possible. Some classic examples are:

- Interrupting the customer. Because you know the answer!
- Constantly trying to add value and participate. Because you can fix the problem!
- Answering questions quickly. Because you are smart and know the answer!
- Not wanting to say, "*I don't know*." Because you don't want to admit that you don't know the answer!
- Proposing a solution too early[10]. Even though you are probably right!
- Making every conversation about your company and technology. Because you are proud of it!
- Listening to respond instead of listening to understand. Because the customer obviously wants and deserves an answer!
- Not sharing knowledge, wisdom, tips, and techniques with your colleagues. Because you want to be "the expert."

You can get to a high S in many ways. Two of the most common are as a new SE, you want to be determined to contribute and can try too hard. Secondly, as an experienced SE, you have all the answers and have already seen almost every problem fifty times. Therefore, you just want to be helpful and share your knowledge. Unfortunately, too much and too little (last bullet point) can give you a poor S score.

Six Ways To Decrease Your Self-Orientation

Yes, I do mean "decrease"! Remember that high S is bad. You want the relationship to be about the customer, not all about you.

1. **Feelings**. As well as going for hard data, try asking the client, "*how do you feel about that?*" It is that touchy-feely area that SEs hate – but it can reveal a lot about what a client is honestly thinking. It's an excellent Intimacy tip as well.

2. **Listen**. Listen really hard. Pause for a second after the client asks you a question to imply thoughtfulness and to ensure that the

---

[10] Labelled by another client as "Premature Solutioneering"!

customer has finished their question. Using non-verbal cues makes the customer feel you have listened and understood. See Chapter 18: The Listening Sales Engineer.

3. **Use *I Don't Know* Wisely (Again).** If you do not know, then you do not know. Promise to find out and give a timeline. If you say, "*I don't know,*" too often, either you or the client is in the wrong meeting. This is a repeat of point #3 for Credibility.

4. Don't fall victim to **Premature Solutioneering.** Even if you know you can help and fix the pain, you must let the client finish talking. Coming up with a solution too quickly can hurt your Credibility, at least until the client has total faith in you. Customers always feel they are unique but secretly hope they are not!

5. **Take The Blame**. It is your fault if something goes wrong or doesn't work or there is a communication failure. That's both internal and external.

6. **Do Right**. Be more concerned about doing the right thing than about being right.

Now complete the fourth scorecard for Self-Orientation. Just another reminder that the scaling is inverted so that a 1 is GOOD and a 5 is BAD.

By now, you may have discovered a strong link between I and S items. However, that relationship becomes even more complex when you add the final factor of Positivity into the equation.

P-Positivity

We all know those people who spend their time looking for problems and issues instead of a healthy balance, which includes opportunities and innovation. You can be a T/A with a low "P" score – many finance, legal, and medical professionals fit into that category. After visiting John, my accountant, I rarely feel uplifted and full of joie de vivre. However, I usually leave the meeting feeling reassured and confident that my taxes are in order and that I will not get in trouble with the myriad of federal, state, and local agencies who each want a piece of our small business. Much of the conversation revolves around either *"Don't do 'x'"* or *"Don't forget to do 'x.'"*

Positivity needs to be authentic. Showing artificial optimism, confidence or spirit can work against you as it is not the "real you." Your body language will betray you, and the false persona will crumble. It's more about looking for the positive, not always focusing on the negativity, and bringing a can-do attitude to the customer. Positivity is not necessarily about being brash, loud, outwardly confident, and smiling. Sales Engineers project a more subtle, but I think deeper, form of quiet confidence.

Many SEs, mainly when speaking with their sales counterparts, can show low Positivity. When you point out the yellow and red lights (warning and danger signs) in an opportunity, highlight the greens as well. You, either personally or collectively as an SE team, do not want to be known as the department of NO. The same applies to working with your clients. Not everything is a problem.

CASE STUDY: I KNOW I SAID NO, BUT...

Paul was a Distinguished Sales Engineer. That's as high a level as an individual contributor could progress in his company and made him the best of the best at the age of just 36. Watching Paul in front of a client was beautiful; you could see how he earned his title. However, watching Paul work with the salespeople back in the office was an entirely different matter.

Over the years, the entire salesforce had turned over, and the average tenure of a rep was now about 12 months. This made Paul rather cynical and a touch arrogant when dealing with his sales counterparts. He said, *"These new reps are just like the hamsters (furry pets) my children keep buying. I don't even bother learning their names anymore, as they just run on the wheel and die after a few months. Why invest in a rep until they've proven themselves and been here at least a year or more?"* This attitude resulted in nothing but Paul lecturing every rep about poor Discovery, the issues with their deals, why they would never win, and it was a waste of his time, etc. Paul's office became a no-fly zone for reps, and no one would speak with him. His deal contribution dried up. He wasn't even the "grumpy old man" as he was only 36 years old.

A Trusted Advisor with clients was now wasted because the salesforce didn't trust him. Paul eventually left the company. He joined a startup, reinvented himself, and rediscovered his passion for all parts of the sales process.

(Although the hamster analogy is terrible, you must admit that the visuals made you smile.)

Six Ways To Increase Your Positivity (In A Positive Way)

1. **Show Appropriate Confidence**. Customers and salespeople hate uncertainty.

2. **Be Optimistic** - with realism. Do not be falsely cheerful, constantly smiling, and say, "*everything will be all right*" when you know it won't. However, I am a big believer in the theory of sales and relationships when one door closes; another door opens. Sometimes you will need to look hard for that open door.

3. **Appreciate Others**. Spend more time recognizing the qualities and achievements of others, whether it is your customers, a salesperson, a partner, a colleague, or even your boss. Don't forget the folks in support, product marketing, and engineering.

4. **AND**. Become a "AND" person instead of a "BUT" person. When someone proposes an idea, try adding to it with an AND[11] instead of countering it with a BUT. This is a fantastic tactic for internal meetings and your personal life.

---

[11] When this book was first released in 2016, two SEs wrote to me and said this was the best piece of advice in the entire book!

5. **Act The Part**. The advice we give to potential first-time managers about *"act like you have the job, dress like you have the job"* applies.

6. **Mentally Rehearse.** When anxious or nervous about a situation, we are all exceptionally talented at thinking about what might go wrong. Take brain time to walk through all the good things that can happen.

Positivity is a smoothing factor that accounts for attitude and other behaviors that didn't fit well into the other four attributes. The default score should be 1.00. You seriously must make a case for why it should change. In the case of Paul, his **P** for clients was probably **1.2**, yet his **P** for internal teamwork was **0.5** (as it so negatively affected everyone else).

Now complete a final score card for Positivity. This card is a little different as it is an overall multiplier. First, define normal business relationships as operating at a **1.00**. Then define behaviours and outcomes at the low end of **0.5** and **0.75** and the high end of **1.2** and **1.33**. In most cases, **1.00** should be the default, and you must have an exceptional reason to go higher or lower. Later in the process, you'll need to avoid the temptation of adjusting P to raise your scores – so be warned.

In Summary

You must understand how the five trust factors apply to you, your job, and your customers. You should now have five completed factor scoresheets (educators call them rubrics) that you can use for the remainder of the book. As you read Section 2, you'll find yourself adding and changing items on the sheets. More help, scoresheets, and a template for an overall scoring sheet are available on the website[12].

---

[12] www.masteringtechnicalsales.com/tabook

THE TRUSTED SALES ENGINEER
WORKSHEET — "T" Scores

Trust Factor	

Score	Your Actions	Customer Actions
1		
2		
3		
4		
5		

Table 2.3: Single Factor Rubric - Scoresheet

Chapter 3: Calculating The Trust Score

N ow, we put all the hard work from the previous chapter to good use. In this chapter, you will calculate a Trust Score (T-Score) for an individual customer and then create a baseline plan to improve your score. To get started, you will need your CRISP scorecard/rubrics from the earlier chapters and the Individual T-Score Worksheet. There is a copy of the worksheet at the end of this chapter and in the MTS Trusted Advisor web area[13].

Getting Started With The T-Score Worksheet

This sheet is the only resource you'll repeatedly see during the T/A process. It is so fundamental that we print it out on bright orange heavy stock paper for our workshops so that you cannot fail to miss its importance.

Step 1:

Select a customer to use as the basis for your first T-Score calculation. Write down their name, title, and company. Once you have completed Section 3 of the book, include their DISC/Colour personality. In this example, borrowed from a client of ours with names changed, they are working with Martin Wainwright (MW), the Operations Director at Acme Rocket Skates Inc[14]. They are a strategic account, yet we have little penetration within Martin's division. There is obviously much work to be done and relationships to be built!

---

[13] Mastering Technical Sales Trusted Advisor Book Content
[14] My beloved fictitious company from the Road Runner Looney Tunes Cartoon series

THE TRUSTED ADVISOR SALES ENGINEER
WORKSHEET – "T" Scores

Customer / Customer Name	Martin Wainwright (MW)	*DISC /*
	Acme Rocketskates	*Colour*
Title / Situation	Operations Director	Blue/Green
	Strategic Account – Little Penetration	

Step 2:

Complete the three columns for each component factor. The first column is your score (from 1 to 5) based on the rubrics you have already created for that factor. The second column is your justification for how/why you achieved that score. It describes the current state to explain the score to your boss or an independent third party. The last column holds your plan for the next 30-60-90 days (you choose) and is your improvement section. Write in the specific steps you will take in the selected period to improve that factor score by at least one point. Focus on the content about intent and behavior rather than beautiful prose and stunning grammar and punctuation.

Factor	Score	Reality - Current State	Actions - Future State
Credibility (1-5)	3	Met MW once. Focused on me vs the rep. Asked many questions. Answered them + suggested alternatives. He followed up on my email.	Follow-up on alternative solutions. Provide references and more detail. Set up solo meeting within 45 days.

In this example, we have a Credibility factor score of **3**. Remember that we deal with integers. Otherwise, the math gets complicated. For this client, **C=3** is the starting point for any SE-Customer relationship. There is no reason after a single meeting for **C** to be anything other than **3**. MW naturally gravitates toward the technician in the room; he asks many questions and then appreciates the responses. He also responded to a follow-up email with a few more questions, which is a good sign. During the next 60 days, the plan to move **C** from **3** up to **4** is for the SE to set up a solo meeting with MW without the rep being present (but aware of the meeting, of course). Plus, come prepared with alternative solutions suggested/mentioned in the discussion.

Step 3:

Repeat the previous step for the remaining three primary factors: Reliability, Intimacy, and Self-Orientation. Although we use a single sheet guide, you can readily expand the sheet into multiple pages, providing exact timelines and way more detail. Also, remember that **S** lives at the bottom of the equation, so reverse the **S** scoring.

Step 4:

Estimate your Positivity factor as an overall multiplier. In most cases P = 1.00. Your scoresheet should now look like this:

Factor	Score	Reality - Current State	Actions - Future State
Credibility (1-5)	3	Met MW once. Focused on me vs the rep. Asked many questions. Answered them + suggested alternatives. He followed up on my email.	Follow-up on alternative solutions. Provide references and more detail. Set up solo meeting within 45 days.
Reliability (1-5)	2	Little chance to demonstrate it. Did respond within 24 hours. Provided him data and metrics he and his team requested.	Need to create opportunities for further interaction. Will also research his org and check his directs for contacts/friends on LinkedIn.
Intimacy (1-5)	2	Single meeting. Don't know much about him. Basic understanding of his biz issues	Research. Find common ground. Send an "in the area" coffee request next week.
Self (5-1)	3	Neutral. He spoke for 75% of the meet so good start. We didn't talk product.	Introduce Steve from our local partner as alternative for services requirement MW mentioned. Have rep suggest contract update to utilize new SAAS rates.
Positivity (0.5-1.33)	1.0	Neutral relationship	Leave as is until my I can improve

Step 5:

Calculate your T-Score using the equation.

(C R I – 1=Poor, 5=Good: S – 1=Good, 5=Poor)

$$T\square\square.\square = \left[\frac{C\square+R\square+I\square}{S\square}\right] * P$$

In this instance, as P= 1.00

$$T\square\square.\square = \left[\frac{C\boxed{3}+R\boxed{2}+I\boxed{2}}{S\boxed{3}}\right] * P$$

So by doing the Math:

T = (3+2+2) / 3 = 7 / 3 = **2.33**

Summary

We have completed a first-pass T-Score calculation. Each successive time you follow the process, it will become faster as you adjust to scoring metrics and basic mathematics. Our very first T-Score attempt yields a number of **2.33**. That opens up many questions. What is a good number? A bad number? What should we aim for in a T-Score? How can we quickly improve our scores? Once we have a score – what do we do with it?

THE TRUSTED SALES ENGINEER
WORKSHEET – "T" Scores

Customer / Customer Name		DISC / Colour
Title / Situation		

Factor	Score	Reality - Current State	Actions - Future State
Credibility (1-5)			
Reliability (1-5)			
Intimacy (1-5)			
Self (5-1)			
Positivity (0.5-1.33)			

Chapter 4: More About The T-Score

Great! We have a T-Score for our first customer – now, what can we do with it? In this chapter, we will dig deeper into the mathematics of the equation and then compare your calculated numbers to industry norms. You will need to add three numbers together, divide that total by a fourth number and perform a piece of simple multiplication. It's not that hard!

Examining The T-Score Numbers

Some simple mathematics shows us the possible maximum, median, and minimum T-score numbers. It's a strange range of results and is by no means linear. For example, the minimum score is 0.3, and the maximum is 20. If you score mid-range on all the factors, you receive a 3.0.

	Score	Mathematical Detail
Minimum T Score	0.3	((1+1+1) / 5) * 0.5
Median T-Score	3.0	((3+3+3) / 3) * 1.0
Maximum T-Score	20.0	((5+5+5) / 1) * 1.33

Table 4.1: Range of T-Scores Using Standardized Scale

Observation shows that **Self-Orientation** is the factor that "moves the trust needle" faster than anything else. That's because it is the equation's denominator (the bottom part). Using the example from the previous chapter, our initial T-Score with Martin Wainwright of Acme Rocket Skates Inc. was 2.33. That is not a bad score at all for a first impression meeting. Using the Trust Improvement Plan over the next 45-60 days, we can see the predicted impact on the T-Score in Table 4.2. For the data people, think of this as sensitivity analysis.

Outcome	Detail + Math	T-Score
Initial Trust Score	(3+2+2) / 3	2.33
Improve R from 2 to 3	(3+3+2) / 3	2.66
Improve C, R, and I by 1	(4+3+3) / 3	3.33
Improve S from 3 to 2	(3+2+2) / 2	3.50
Improve all factors by 1	(4+3+3) / 2	5.00
Continued Improvement	(5+5+4) / 2	7.00
And Reduce S to 1	(5+5+4)/ 1	14.00

Table 4.2: Improvement of T-Score In Various Situations

In this example, an improvement in **S** by just 1 point outweighs improving **C+R+I** by one point apiece. Improving each factor by a point more than doubles our score. So, when in doubt – focus on the **S** and ensure you get that right, as it's the most critical part of improving the equation. We will see the necessity of doing that in Chapter 25 – Your Trusted Advisor Profile. As a quick preview of the data, most SEs rate **S** as one of their weaker skills[15].

Calibrating The T-Score

We can now estimate how to correlate your T-Score to your Trusted Advisor status based on data gathered from over fifty companies in the high technology industry. Of course, each company builds its scorecard differently, so a T=5 at Cisco may be slightly different than that used within parts of Red Hat or Oracle, or a small single product startup.

Use the numbers from Table 4.3 as guidelines, as your results may vary. Most inter-company variations are caused by using either a 2 or a 3 as baseline "standard business behavior" for C, R, I, and S.

---

[15] Which seems strange. Further analysis shows it is rated as weaker because although most SE's have low S, they're confused how to show it. That is more confidence than skill.

Range T-Score	Standard Result / Outcomes
< 2	Poor – Minimal Trust and No Relationship
2-4	Standard Relationship – Friendly, But Not Deep
4-5	Will start to sell and promote you internally (if low risk to themselves)
5-7	Good solid relationship – customer will take action and do things for you that have some risk.
7-10	Trusted Advisor I
10+	Trusted Advisor II

Table 4.3: Trusted Advisor Scoring Ranges and Interpretation

Our initial run-through with the Martin Wainwright example provided a score of **2.33**, a typical initial relationship score. It is businesslike but not particularly deep. If you asked Martin to do you a favour or to introduce you to the executive suite, he'd be unlikely to comply, and your T-Score may actually drop because you made that request.

By following through on your plan and increasing each Trust factor by a point, that **2.33** becomes a **5.00.** Martin is now far more likely to assist you, share additional information, and possibly guide you through the organization.

With considerably more effort in improving the (C+R+I) top line total, your T-Score can climb to a **7.00**, which puts you in Trusted Advisor territory. You can now consider Martin your internal coach, opening doors for you within the company, pushing your projects, and acting as an excellent reference. Of course, in return for all this help, you must continue to provide value back to Martin.

A final step in this story is now to reduce your S factor from a 2 to 1. This intuitively doubles your score to **14.0,** and you operate in the rarefied air of a Trusted Advisor II or Master Advisor. You fully engage with your client's short- and long-term strategy, can visit the client at short notice, and offer advice on multiple areas outside your (and possibly your company's) domain of expertise and knowledge.

Using The T-Score In Technical Account Planning

It may be enough for some SEs to have a methodology to define and measure Trust just for measurement and monitoring. However, the effectiveness in a sales organization occurs during Technical Account Planning. A significant part of such planning revolves around the client personnel you need to interact with – both those you know and those you do not (yet) know. This area is where the T-Scores come into play. Look at the organizational chart or list of client personnel and write down your T-Score (if you have one) with them. The salesperson and anyone else engaged in the account should do the same. When you need to approach a specific individual to take a course of action, see who has the highest T-Score. That is who should make the request. It is a big difference from the typical *"SE takes the techies, and salesrep takes the execs"* strategy.

The problematic piece of calibration comes in judging what your score needs to be to take a course of action. That is something you will need to discover by some trial and error and common sense.

Mini-Exercise 4.1 Self-Calibration

Make a list of common tasks and actions during a sales cycle and assign the minimum T-Score required for the client to respond positively. Some examples might be:

- ✓ Act As A Reference
- ✓ Short-Cut An RFP
- ✓ Act As A Press Reference
- ✓ Agree To A Custom Demo Instead Of A POC
- ✓ Walk You Into The Office Of Their Immediate Manager/Boss
- ✓ Provide You With Competitive Information
- ✓ Introduce You To A Corporate Executive
- ✓ Walk You Across To A Peer in Another Department

Summary

In four chapters, we have created a basic working definition of Trust and Advice, built a Trust measurement scale, and then measured T-Scores with a sample client. That's all been a little abstract and has mainly reflected what you think and how you act. The content and examples within the remaining chapters in Section 1 should now help you refine your measurement scale and give you ideas about how to construct a Trust Improvement Plan with almost anyone.

Remember that the scoring mechanism and the T-Scores are only approximations and guidelines for the state of your client relationships and Trusted Advisor Status. When in doubt about taking a course of action or making a customer request, first apply your common sense.

Chapter 5: The Customer Point Of View

As stated earlier, your customer is the only person who matters in the entire Trusted Advisor journey. It does not matter what you think or call yourself – the customer counts. That customer has a lot of "sales noise" to cut through regarding communications from their vendors through various media and mechanisms. It is getting worse – when I started as a SE, all I had to worry about was telephone calls, paper mail, and physical meetings!

CASE STUDY – YOU ARE ALL THE SAME

As an IT executive, I once asked my assistant to track the number of external meeting requests I received in a month. Over three months, the average was 122, which was well before social media kicked in as a communications channel. Of those 122, I met with 5 - 8 a month, depending on which projects were in progress and if anyone really got my attention. The interesting data from a Trusted Advisor point of view is that the percentage of vendors who wanted to be my "business partner" was 100%. However, the percentage who told me how they would do that (other than giving me a great price) was less than 5%.

So What Does the Customer Really Want From The SE?

A few years ago, I was in the audience at one of my client's annual sales kickoff events. On stage was someone from McKinsey, the well-respected management consulting company, giving some bland predictions about the future of technology sales and the needs of large enterprise customers. The one idea I did come away with was that no one with a SE background had ever asked commercial customers precisely what they wanted and valued from <u>their</u> vendor SE teams. So with a mental assist from McKinsey, we gathered that data over almost a year and continue to collect it at every opportunity.

The fundamental question asked was, *"what are the skills you value most from your vendor's sales engineering team?"* Although we had to explain precisely what sales engineering was a few times, we gathered over 2,000 responses from mid-level managers and executives spanning 20 countries and multiple lines of business and IT units. The top five responses were:

Rank	Skill
#1	Someone who understands my business
#2	Someone who can design innovative solutions with my staff
#3	Someone who I can trust to do the right things for us
#4	Someone who can communicate effectively with me
#5	Someone with deep technical knowledge

Table 5.1: Top Skills Requested By Customers (April 2021)

The top four responses gathered a solid score of over 80% from the surveyed group. Response #5 – deep technical knowledge – scored just over 50%. Another dozen responses made up the tail, scoring from 25% down to the single digits. Deep technical skills are now just table stakes. It's what your customers expect you to bring into a relationship as part of your job. What matters most to them is how you use that knowledge, as shown by the four attributes that score above it. My favorite write-in response was, *"solve more problems than your company creates"*!

So let's look at those top five responses in a little more detail as they relate to the Trust factors.

#1 – Someone Who Understands My Business

Customers don't expect you to know the everyday minutiae of their business, but they hope that you understand the big picture and industry trends and share what others might be doing. As a specific example, when dealing with the research arm of a pharmaceutical company, you should understand how the clinical trial process works, the impact of regulatory agencies, and how time to market (in terms of patent protection) is a key business driver. That translates to raised Credibility and Intimacy and a lowered Self as the conversation is about them and not about you.

#2 – Someone Who Can Design Innovative Solutions With My Staff

Note the phrasing in this attribute. The "innovative" adjective came through loud and clear, as does the "with" modifier. Your customer is looking for collaboration, plus some education and teaching, and not just a pre-packaged solution. That is the value add of the Sales Engineer. That translates to high Credibility, Intimacy to work with and assist the client team, and a healthy dose of Positivity to convince them, in many cases, that what you are proposing will work.

#3 – Someone I Can Trust To Do The Right Thing

If that phrase is not an excellent summary of a Trusted Advisor, I don't know what is. Customers repeatedly told us that they were tired of being sold something that did not necessarily benefit them as much as it should have. On many occasions, there were alternate and cheaper or more flexible options they could have chosen with the correct guidance. All five factors come into play on this attribute, although I would make the case that Credibility, Intimacy, and Self lead the pack.

#4 – Someone Who Can Communicate Effectively With Me

You may be the most capable and innovative SE in the world, but if you cannot explain your ideas and thinking to the people who count – it all amounts to nothing. Unfortunately, far too many SEs are so proud of their technical capabilities (see next point) that they lose sight of the fact that you must be able to speak, present, listen and communicate to be effective. I've always struggled with the Trust factors on this point. However, if you wrap everything with attitude (i.e. Positivity) and understand enough about your customer (Intimacy), you can get the idea across.

An alternative perspective to the rating of this response is presented by CEB – the creators of The Challenger Sale[16]. Their research shows that *"Being Easy To Understand'* and even *"Representing a Smart/Expert Perspective"* have minimal impact when engaged in their Challenger philosophy. But, of course, that data is for salespeople rather than Sales Engineers – nonetheless interesting.

#5 – Someone With Deep Technical Knowledge

In many T /A workshops, we first give the participants the choice of prioritizing the five attributes. They often place the "#3-Trust" and "#5-Technical Knowledge" above everything else. It is frequently a shock when it scores poorly and comes in fifth place. This ranking shows how the role of the SE and the SE-salesperson interaction has changed over the past 30 years. It used to be that deep technical knowledge was enough to ensure you a job as a Senior SE for life, but not anymore. This attribute is primarily driven by Credibility. It is also worth noting that as you move further down the corporate org chart towards the individual contributor, the more valuable deep technical knowledge will become. For example, the network engineer or database administrator will value your knowledge more than their CIO. The CIO will appreciate it because it can help her staff, but she is still much more interested in the other four attributes at a professional level.

Mini-Exercise #5.1: Some Trusted Introspection

Now reflect on those five top attributes and write down your preferred order based on your customers. If you think there is something even more important, feel free to add it to the list (I will not be offended). Then think about your interactions with those customers over the past few months – has that been your priority? How well has that relationship developed? Is there anything you can do in the next 4-6 weeks to switch or improve your priorities to match your customers?

---

[16] https://www.challengerinc.com/sales . And it is a philosophy rather than a process.

We will revisit these five attributes in a later chapter, but for now, take note of the minimal impact of Reliability compared to Credibility, Intimacy, Self, and Positivity.

In Summary

You now have some research and insight into what the customer expects from you. Keep the five customer requirements in mind as you read through the chapters and complete the exercises. If what you are doing does not positively contribute to at least one of those attributes, it's unlikely to contribute towards raising your trust scores.

Chapter 6: A Little More About Trust

Trust(ed): (a) Reliance on the integrity, strength, ability, surety, etc., of a person or thing; confidence. (b) Confident expectation of something; hope. (c) Something committed or entrusted to one's care for use or safekeeping, as an office, duty, or the like; responsibility; charge.

My grandfather, George William Care, was a man with little formal education and a massive amount of common sense and everyday wisdom. He had two favorite pieces of advice that have stuck with me over the years. The first (which has nothing to do with being a Trusted Advisor, but I'll share anyway) was, *"Business is like a wheelbarrow. It only moves when you push it."* The second more pertinent piece of advice was, *"A man's trust has to be earned. And once you earn that trust, you must work just as hard to keep it."*

Trust, both in the personal and business spheres of your life, does not suddenly spring into existence. For example, after a single meeting, a customer is not likely to say, *"I trust her,"* but is likely to feel (even if they don't yet realize it) that she is a person they may be able to trust at some future point. When that eventually happens lies in the mechanics of the developing relationship, yet a solid first impression supplies an excellent basis to build trust.

CASE STUDY – MY FIRST SE JOB

After my wife and I moved to the US, my very first job as an SE was for a company called Mathematica, based in Princeton, New Jersey. We sold what was then called a Fourth Generation Reporting Language. Our product RAMIS competed against FOCUS (which is still around today and sold by Information

Builders). Although I got to work with 4-5 reps in my first few months, I was privileged to collaborate with Linda Weber. Linda had been a successful rep for the past few years and was not much older (although she was way more experienced) than me. I was a total SE novice. I knew the product, but other than some rudimentary sales training, I had no idea how to demo, present, or behave.

I quickly learnt over the subsequent half-dozen sales calls that if Linda asked me to do something, regardless of the deadline or the apparent usefulness of my actions, I did it because she needed it done to get a deal. I noted that she always briefed me on the sales meetings, explained exactly what she knew, what she did not, what the objectives of the call were – and my role. Then, which won over my loyalty and trust, she asked me (a complete beginner) what I thought about her strategy and listened to my poorly reasoned input.

Trust grows and develops as a relationship grows. I believe it reaches a point when, no matter what Grandpa said, the trust is fixed and is here to stay without much maintenance and upkeep. However, for most relationships, especially those still growing, you have to work at it. This applies to your customers, the salespeople you work with and keep out of trouble, your peers, and your managers, and especially to the non-sales departments in your company like development, support, or marketing. You need them in order to perform your job as efficiently as possible.

Trust, Risk, Logic, and Emotion

Another exciting perspective about trust is that it involves some degree of risk – both from an emotional / personal point of view and from a clear and factual/logical view. For one person to trust another, there is an element of risk. For example, when a customer trusts that your recommended configuration is the best, he is taking a risk. That's both a professional business risk in that you are indeed correct and the design will function cost-effectively, but also a personal risk in that you aren't deceiving him and won't make him look stupid, gullible, or lose face in front of others.

That usually means the SE must give something in the relationship to build trust. Although the customer may sometimes confide in you or provide some insider information, that is rarely done in isolation or on the first contact unless there is some other motive. You need to start the process by sharing some information or private part of yourself. Back in my Mathematica days, whenever I had to go onsite and install our software (this was pre-web and even pre-CD), I always shared a story with the Systems Programmer about how I had messed up my very first install. I accidentally skipped from page 4 to page 6 and missed all the tuning options. I discovered that sharing some mishaps, even with the most data-driven logical data center tech, helped humanize me and was a good starting point to build a "techie" bond. That may not have done much for my Credibility and Reliability, but it certainly influenced my Intimacy and Self-Orientation.

Looking at that in retrospect, from a logical/factual point of view, I was admitting that I made mistakes, yet from an emotional perspective, I was a "regular" person as we all make mistakes. A different example might be that I trust John, my accountant, as he has been consistently correct and accurate in the past – that's the logical/factual mindset. However, with all due respect to CPAs, they are not always the most scintillating and extrovert people, and from a personal/emotional point of view, I don't know much about him. Now John would say that he wants me to trust him as a professional CPA and not as a person, but somehow, I feel the two need to be intertwined.

CASE STUDY – THE SINGAPORE SLING

My business partners in Singapore are two ex-pat Aussies – Tom King and Nick Dorney. They now represent Mastering Technical Sales in Asia-Pacific and sell my material and content to high-tech companies in that part of the world. We formed our partnership based on a couple of phone calls and a few Skype sessions. There was a lot of trust extended on both sides. In effect, I trusted them with some of my Intellectual Property and that they would fairly pay me when making a sale and delivering workshops. They trusted that my content was high quality, that I'd train their delivery team, and that I wouldn't sell into the Asia-Pacific region through the US headquarters of my customer base and cut them out of a deal. We formed the partnership on a virtual handshake and a ridiculously short and simple legal agreement.

It's been a fantastic success for all concerned. We now deliver MTS materials in multiple languages and 20 countries throughout Asia – all on the same handshake and two pages of paper. Both sides indeed extended their trust, and we both had to give a lot to get back even more.

Mini-Exercise #6.1: Who Do You Trust And Why?

Just because someone says, *"Trust Me!"* does not mean that you should - it might even cause the opposite reaction. So, look around you at work and in your home life. Aside from some obvious family members, who do you trust? Why is that? How long have you trusted them, and has that trust grown and ebbed over the years or stayed constant? Keep this list; you'll also need it in Chapter 26 – The Trusted Advisor At Home.

CASE STUDY: THE LUCK OF THE IRISH

Niall and Siobhan (blame their parents if you have issues with pronunciation) were the top performing Sales-SE team for the Dublin office of a global software company. They did not have the best territory, they did not have the richest and free-spending accounts, and they certainly weren't the most experienced members of the Irish office. Yet, after the first 12 months featuring a lot of hard work, they were the #1 team for the next four years. The secret to their success was trust. Trust between the two of them and the trust of their customers. Early in their relationship, the two of them decided to trust that the other person knew what they were doing, and they set themselves a mission of minimizing the number of two-headed, four-legged calls they made. Obviously, there were many occasions when they needed to work together in the same room, yet Niall trusted that Siobhan could work the technical side of the house. Siobhan trusted that Niall could manage Business Discovery and Needs Analysis without her. As a result, they practically doubled the call productivity of every other team.

In Summary

In wrapping this chapter, it is essential to emphasize the distinction between trust between two individuals and trust between an individual and an organization or profession. Despite the old line from the 1960s of *"never trust anyone over 30, or from the government"*, organizational trust is a perceptual emotion. For example, we naturally trust nurses and doctors far more than salespeople, lawyers, and politicians –a global phenomenon. As Sales Engineers, we have an advantage over the Salespeople we work with (see Chapter 8). If we behave appropriately, we are viewed as technical doctors or nurses who can fix problems and alleviate (business) pain. Politicians and lawyers can fend for themselves!

Chapter 7: A Little More About Advice And Advisors

Advice: Guidance or recommendations concerning prudent future action, typically given by someone regarded as knowledgeable or authoritative.

Advisor: (a) One who gives <u>advice</u>. **(b)** a teacher responsible for <u>advising</u> students on academic matters. **(c)** a fortuneteller.

Sales Engineers love to provide advice. We freely advise our clients, often ignoring whether they ask for it or not. We freely advise salespeople about how to qualify better deals (whether they ask for it or not), and we advise the Engineering team about ways to make the product better (who hardly ever will ask for advice). We advise our peers about better ways to demo, present and work with customers. The common theme behind each of those examples is that advice is a two-way street. Someone must provide advice, yet even more importantly, someone has to listen and accept it. Anyone can give advice, and that does not make you an advisor. The key is that your advice must be accepted, and someone must take action.

Trust has a logical and emotional component, yet giving and taking advice has those same components. So please forget about the fortune-telling option for now.

Mini-Exercise #7.1: Who Do You Trust And Why?

Examine some situations you may have encountered over the past 12 months. Think about the following situations and examine why you acted the way you did and the ramifications of your decision. Finally, make a judgement about the degree of trust you placed in that individual before and after they supplied advice.

    A. Has someone given you good advice that you ignored? Why?
    B. Has someone given you good advice that you accepted? Why?
    C. Has someone given you terrible advice that you accepted? Why?

Delivering The Advice

On many occasions, the primary decision about whether to accept or reject advice does not relate to the quality of the advice. Instead, especially in the SE world, where we can assume that the majority of your advice is sound and well-reasoned, it all comes down to the delivery of the advice. So yes – it's all about how you give advice and make it easy for the customer to accept and execute upon that advice. Although part of being a T/A is to have a difficult conversation that no one else may be willing to conduct, that is not the default communications mechanism, as this story will illustrate.

CASE STUDY – BEING RIGHT, AND BEING RIGHT

Melissa was a young, rising star Sales Engineer who had moved from the consulting ranks into Sales Engineering the previous year. She was undoubtedly both personable and knowledgeable. Her one issue was that she carried her straightforward consulting manners into the SE role.

Five weeks into the job, Melissa went onsite and conducted a "health check" for an existing customer. The purpose was to see how well they had set up and optimized their system. She discovered a lot of room for improvement. Her delivery of those results started with, and I paraphrase this to make it gentler than it actually was, *"Here are my findings showing that your system is poorly configured and a list of two dozen things you screwed up that we can help you fix.*

52

The result is that we can double the throughput of your system by eliminating all these errors".

She sat back, expecting praise. Instead, the IT Director smiled politely, took a copy of her report, and said, *"Thank you. We'll study these recommendations and let you know how we'll want to proceed".* It took us a year of groveling and apologizing to get back into the account. Also, note that the client did, of course, make the recommended changes all by themselves.

Breaking down the delivery of advice and subsequent acceptance when looking at the Trust Factors yields some interesting results. Credibility is obviously a requirement, as the customer does need to believe in both you and what you are saying. Reliability takes more of a back seat on this one. Intimacy is vital. If you cannot deliver the advice in a format that the customer will accept and process, then almost everything else is pointless. Self is also a leading indicator, as the client needs to feel that you are looking out for them and not providing them with a self-serving recommendation. Positivity also leaps into play as a display of confidence linked to the Intimacy factor helps "set" the advice into the client's mindset. Just as a practical example, if someone I trust tells me that I "have to" take a course of action, it's likely that I will dig my heels in and resist, <u>even if I know they are right</u>! (My wife and children know this very well). However, if that same person says, *"John, we have a couple of options here – let's run through them and see what you think."* they will get me to listen and probably take the course of action they recommend – because I have input and choice.

Extend that to the SE role when a customer asks you for advice.

Customer: *"How would you recommend we implement your solution?"*

SE: *"Well, Ms. Customer, based on what I know about your environment, there seems to be a couple of ways to do it. Let me walk you through those options, and we can come up with an initial decision."*

(Note that the customer does not want to hear that your product is so flexible that there are 29 ways of doing it. That will scare them and extend

53

your sales cycle. Your job is to close down options and guide the customer, not confuse them with too many choices).

The final and more general aspect of advice is that it must be understandable and relevant.

Understandable comes from overcoming The Curse Of Knowledge[17]. This is a situation when you live and breathe the use and application of your product/solution/service every single working day. In many cases, this is all new to your customer, or they have cursory knowledge at best. Do not assume that they know as much as you think they should. It often helps to ask at what level to pitch your answers or descriptions. Also, do not assume that the customer will automatically understand. Relevance comes from just sharing enough information with the customer so that they can internalize your advice.

Recently I watched a security SE answer a question with an amazing in-depth explanation of Next-Generation Firewalls. It was a beautiful and very technically accurate three minutes – and totally missed the mark as the person who asked the question was a non-technical process individual from Compliance.

CASE STUDY – THE TEACHER'S STORY

My beloved wife, Allison, taught Fifth Grade students – which to readers outside the U.S. means 10-11-year-old children. I've found that over the years, I have learnt a lot from studying what she studies – notably when she received her Master's degree. One of the modules in a Classroom Management workshop was about the power of positivity and placing yourself, as the teacher, in a position of failure rather than the students. That all sounded a little new age touchy-feely to me until I saw some practical examples. Instead of saying, *"does everyone understand that?"* in class after reviewing part of a lesson, you say, *"did I make that clear?"* The first version puts pressure on the student to say that they didn't understand, whilst the second version puts pressure on the teacher for not

---

[17] The Curse Of Knowledge by Chip and Dan Heath : https://hbr.org/2006/12/the-curse-of-knowledge

clearly explaining. It's a minor point, but when I implemented this in my workshops some 10-12 years ago and suggested the technique to my other instructors, we noted a sizable increase in questions.

Just think about that next time you explain a technical feature or function.[18]

We'll look at the situational aspects of giving and accepting advice a lot more in Section 2, but at this point, I'll ask that if you didn't try the mini-exercise towards the start of this chapter, you now go back and run through it.

In Summary

It is all about finding a way to give advice that is listened to and ultimately acted upon[19]. Unfortunately, there is no room within a T/A vocabulary for phrases such as *"I told you so!"* Therefore, the burden is on you to deliver the correct advice that checks off both the emotional and logical acceptance criteria for your clients.

---

[18] You can also, especially in a virtual environment say "what questions do you have for me" instead of "any questions"!

[19] Ending sentences with a preposition. See http://public.wsu.edu/~brians/errors/churchill.html

Chapter 8: The Built-In Advantage Of A Sales Engineer

"Always do right. This will gratify some people and astonish the rest."

- Mark Twain

One of the best things about being a Sales Engineer (think of it as a "feature") is that we have many advantages compared to others within our company. That is because we can bring knowledge and value into a conversation. A survey reproduced below really reinforces that statement. We now have over 6,100 responses worldwide to support the SE Value Proposition.

Throughout your technology purchase process, which of these sources/groups provided the most value to you and your team? (%) values			
Customer Position	Middle Management	IT - Individuals	CxO / Executives
General Collateral	25.1	22.6	16.2
Salesperson/ Manager	21.3	18.8	22.6
Technical Team	39.7	46.8	42.1
Executives	13.9	11.8	19.1

Table 8.1: The Value Of A Sales Engineer (Source: Mastering Technical Sales 4th Edition Research. 8019 responses through April 2021)

Here is the thought experiment. You and a salesperson walk into the office of a mid-to senior-level decision-maker at one of your customers. In the absence of any other meaningful or pre-existing relationship, who will that customer naturally trust more – you or the salesperson? It's **YOU**.

Why? Because the salesperson is there to sell the customer something. Which is OK as that is their job. You gain in trust level simply by comparison to the salesperson. That is not bad and reflects on the sales profession rather than the individual rep. However, it is an advantage for you to capitalize upon, and it is an advantage that can quickly and rapidly disappear.

You Are There To Help The Customer

Your job as a Trusted Advisor (and just as a good Sales Engineer) is to help the customer, allowing the salesperson to "sell" the customer. Your best strategy is to ask some great questions, listen to the answers and then process the information. Then you provide some insight and recommendations based on that information. Listening is one of the premier and most challenging skills for a SE to develop and master.

One of your toughest tasks is usually allowing the customer to speak without interruption. Either by you or by other members of your sales team. They must trust that you know what you are doing and have the competency to run a meeting.

The instant you explicitly try to sell something, transparently apply a marketing spin on an issue, or even go into sales mode by directly asking about budget or timelines, that trust may disappear[20]. Once an SE loses a customer's trust, it is incredibly hard to win it back. Next to lying, going over to "The Dark Side" of salesmanship is the leading cause of SE trust deterioration.

---

[20] Of course an SE can ask about time and/or money. That works best in a 1:1 situation and phrased so that both parties gain a benefit.

Absolute and Reflected Trust

Looking at this in terms of the Trust Equation, you have an implied high Credibility score as you are the technical part of the team. Your Reliability is about the same as the salespersons – as most reps are responsive to customers, and it is easy to show. The rep may have an edge in Intimacy through sheer personality, although if you have done a little research about the customer, that soon balances out. Self-Orientation gives you a significant advantage as your intent to help instead of sell will come through in your voice, body language, and actions. Although the expert salesperson can balance that with appropriate behavior and "I" is the weakest trait of the standard SE anyway.

The decision you need to make, not just for an initial meeting but also for subsequent calls when your T score is higher than the reps, is how much trust to loan or reflect back, on the salesperson. Anytime you tell the customer, or even imply it, that the rep is someone who can be trusted ("he's a good guy"), you are putting your T score, and specifically your Credibility and Reliability, at risk.

It's your decision. Personally, when I worked with a rep who had been around for a while, had a good reputation and some experience, I'd loan her some trust. Contrast that with a recently recruited 25-year-old MBA, eager to please his 27-year-old sales manager, who both thought they could revolutionize sales – not so much! Yet this is a situation that many transactional-oriented SEs in an SMB or Inside Sales unit encounter every month.

CASE STUDY – THE EIGHT-FOLD PATH TO BECOMING A TRUSTED ADVISOR

Chris Daly, former VP of Sales Engineering at Symantec, has an insightful and amusing story about utilizing trust and the different levels of trust for a Sales Engineer. *"An SE on my team was assigned to DHL/Americas when they were trying to take share from UPS and FedEx. This SE and I worked through his process on how he gained T/A status, and it was all about "access." With apologies to the Buddhist concept of the "Eight–Fold Path to Enlightenment," we called this the "Eight–Fold Path to becoming a Trusted Advisor."*

---

1. **Access to the Building** – he'd camp in the lobby until someone saw him and asked him to come on in!

2. **Access to a Badge** – allowing him to come and go as he pleased.

3. **Access to the People** –assigned a cubicle or shared cubicle and posting consistent office hours

4. **Access to the Peoples' Problems** – whether they had anything to do with our offerings or not.

5. **Access to the Table where the problems were discussed and solved.** - and being a contributor to the solution strategy.

6. **Access to the Person** who had the budget to solve the problem by implementing the solution strategy

7. **Access to that Person's Peers and Executives** with other and potentially more significant problems.

8. **Root Access!**

Michael, the SE, gained unprecedented access to both the America's CIO and the Global CIO board and was sought after for solution architectures for some of their most demanding scalability strategies to take on market share. Plus, as his Director, I was invited to DHL's quarterly reviews giving me access too. We were the standard that all other suppliers were held up against, including those receiving significantly more spending. "Deal of the Year," "SE of the Year," "Highest Overachievers," all those accolades that come from significant success followed."

Leveraging The Trust Advantage

You should absolutely use this built-in advantage for your company's good – as long as it ultimately helps the customer. There are several ways to capitalize on this:

1. **Information Flow**. Customers will tell you things they would never tell the salesperson. You can learn about internal politics, competition, personal wins, and many other items. This is the #1 reason to have meetings and conversations without the rep being

around and is a major advantage of physical versus virtual meetings. Hence the old SE saying: *"You can't buy a customer a beer on a webcast."*[21]

2. **Information Flow #2**. It works two ways! Your customers – notably senior execs and purchasing agents - will ask you questions to solicit information that the rep would never disclose. Be careful – and ask the rep what to say about discounts, legal terms, or product futures. The best approach is to plead ignorance.

3. **Laying The Competitive Trap**. Dropping a competitive advantage into the conversation is easy when the Trust Equation is in your favor. A simple statement like *"my customers tell me that the ability to have 'reverse osmotic network regeneration' is the number #1 thing they like as it saves them hours of time each month."* Done. No salesperson can do that with the same level of believability.

4. **Switching Hats**. There are ways to gather additional qualification information without sounding like a rep. It is OK to ask these questions under certain circumstances in small groups. Especially if the sales rep doesn't qualify, is afraid to ask a tricky question, or is part of your account strategy. For example, you can frame a question about project timing around implementation or product availability.

   a. You: *"Steve – when are you hoping to go live with this project? I'm trying to decide on some implementation and deployment recommendations, and that info would help me give you a better answer."*
   b. You: *"Steve – can you share with me just an approximate budget? That would help me to frame the best solution / architecture / project plan for you based on what I've seen over the past few years."*

---

[21] Upended by the events of early 2020 and Covid-19.

In each scenario, you are framing the question with the perspective of gaining information that would help the customer and benefit you—a perfect win-win.

THE LUCK OF THE IRISH – PART TWO

Returning to the story of Niall and Siobhan from the earlier chapter, they also spent a lot of time analyzing who could develop the best relationships with their key customer contacts. They abandoned the classic "*SE takes the Techies, and Sales takes the Business and CxO's*" strategy and went with whatever was easier. This approach led to Siobhan building a lasting relationship with the CIO of a large media company that resulted in being the first ever vendor invited to their annual strategic offsite meeting. That, in turn, resulted in a multi-million-euro contract about six months later. Niall freely admits that he would never have been invited to that meeting or even been able to obtain the invitation for Siobhan to attend. Not to be outdone, Niall cultivated a relationship with a senior network engineer at another client based on a shared love of cycling. He learnt about a competitor trying to undercut them through a US contract and took appropriate action.

In Summary

Trust is hard to gain and easy to lose, so treat it like a natural and not-so-renewable resource. Don't be afraid to leverage your built-in trust advantage against that of the rep, the sales manager, and even your own executives, as it is YOU the customers want to see. Just make sure that everyone looks good, as you cannot destroy the credibility of a salesperson to increase yours.

Chapter 9: And What Do Sales Think About This?

nitially, not that much! This is a classic situation of accepting some short-term pain to obtain some significant longer-term gains. There is no question that sales-oriented issues and concerns arise during the initial phases of a T/A program. Section 3 will examine some of the implementation issues, but we'll look at three of the immediate sales implications here.

1. Some deals will slip to the next quarter.
2. Other deals will disappear from the early pipeline stages.
3. The pipeline will start to increase in size.

So Pretend You Are a Salesperson

The underlying challenge is that salespeople are usually keen to start a "Trusted Advisor" program for their larger clients (although you could argue that it is not a "program," it is an attitude and eventually a natural habit) until they realize the implications. That is not a negative against salespeople when you reflect upon their job's incentives and compensation package structure. Commercial companies pay their salespeople to move a transaction from the start to the end of the pipeline as quickly as possible, simultaneously meeting a monthly or quarterly sales target. Considering that industry statistics show only 60% of reps[22] achieved their goals, closing the deal within a specific mandated timeframe is everything for many reps.

---

[22] The Sales Performance Institute says 59%, and Accenture claims 66%.

Left to their natural tendencies, only about 20% of a salesforce want to embrace a T/A program as initially described to them. A middle band of 40-50% is willing to try once they have been "sold" on a program, and the remaining group will stubbornly resist. Sometimes, they are doing well enough and don't want to change. In others, it is pure resistance to something new and different that potentially takes things out of their control. I've also seen that senior management cannot mandate a T/A program to Sales. Instead, the Sales Engineering team needs to "sell" them with the full and vocal support of all levels of Sales Management.

First-line Sales Management is the key to the success of the program.

When the first-line managers resist and provide either active or passive-aggressive resistance to the program – it will fail except for small pockets of local success. It does not matter what anyone else in the organization says or does.

Let's go back to those three issues:

1. *Some Deals Will Slip Into The Next Quarter* This will happen as you examine more of the "forecasted" deals in detail and have the courage to ask some qualifying and disqualifying questions. You will also discover that you can make some deals larger (by adding in additional projects / requirements / functions), but that may cause the deal to push out by a month or two.

2. *Other Deals Will Totally Disappear From The Early Pipeline Stages.* Many "fluff" and "maybe" deals will disappear as you start having honest and straightforward conversations with your customers. This often ties in with the reduction of RFPs that you need to process. You'll also be able to have more focused and meaningful timeline conversations with the customer that will help you forecast the timing of pipeline deals.

3. *The Pipeline Will Start To Increase In Size.* As part of the Trusted Advisor position, you'll gain a better insight into your customer's future plans and vision. This is the opposite of point #2. For almost

every deal that will disappear from the pipeline, you'll gain one back (our data says 1.2x when measured by revenue) that is far more grounded in reality and will have a higher and more confident closure probability.

CASE STUDY: EVERY CLOUD HAS A (LARGE) SILVER LINING

Steven had the same large account in his territory for three years. Although he managed to obtain business from them every year and had a friendly relationship with his client, he was viewed as a supplier of technology more than a business partner. So after mapping out his connections and those of his SE, he set out to improve his T-Scores.

Not much happened for many months until he was summoned into the office of the senior purchasing agent. He was informed that they were issuing an RFP for some infrastructure software and that his company was not considered. He immediately started to protest. The purchasing agent held up his hand to stop him in his tracks. *"But,"* added the client, *"We have a large new initiative in one of our subsidiaries that seems perfect for your company. If you think you can handle it, make a proposal, and if it is a fit, the business is yours"*.

In Summary

You will naturally encounter some resistance from the sales team when implementing a T/A program. It is viewed as an impediment to existing deals and unnecessary work or effort between an incoming lead and a contract signature. Expect skepticism. We will look at some implementation strategies in Section 3. However – the next section deals with the realities and practicality of becoming a T/A when conducting your everyday SE activities. You are more in control of those activities than anyone else – so now it's up to you!

Section 2: Putting It Into Practice

"The trick to gain customer trust is to avoid all tricks."

Jerry Weinberg, Author/Consultant

This section covers the actual activities an SE performs daily and looks at their implications. Your homework and mission, should you accept it, is to build a list of "do and don't" behaviors for each trust factor. Making a list isn't too hard. It's the application of the list that is tougher. Think of it as creating a general relationship and job improvement action plan; it is up to you (and maybe your boss, with some help from your loved ones) to assist you in implementing it.

That last sentence is worth unpacking. Although you are responsible for your career and performance, many people can help you. I arbitrarily choose your boss and your loved ones because they have a personal interest in your self-improvement. My wife, Allison, was all over my plan to improve my listening skills and was willing to let me practice as much as I wanted! There is nothing new in sharing your goals so that other people can help you and hold you accountable if you stop trying or falter in achieving those goals. If you keep them a secret, you are attempting to be a Trusted Advisor to yourself. It may work, but it's a low probability approach.

So - back to the specific behavioral changes. At the end of the next chapter, there is an outline table to complete to list your intended changes and reinforcing behavior. This is when you must put in most of the work. Convert the tips, techniques, and ideas into specific actions that work for you. You can find an electronic copy of this worksheet, and all the others, at: www.masteringtechnicalsales.com/tabook

Chapter 10: Conversations And Customer Engagement

Most chapters of this section deal with specific parts of the sales cycle. However, we start with a more general aspect of the sales cycle, which occurs through the process – simply having a client conversation. Extending this a little more, especially when working on the Intimacy side of things, the conversation may not even be deal related. Unless you feel the client is trying to avoid discussing a particular subject with you, a meaningful non-work-related conversation is usually a good thing.

To state the simple and the obvious – it is a conversation, which implies a two-way communication of words, emotions, and ideas. There is no such thing as a one-way conversation as that implies a type of lecture, rant, or sermon. Even if someone is pouring out their frustrations, hopes, and dreams to you, you are still interacting with them and making affirmations and summaries.

Some General Conversational Guidelines.

1. **Make It About The Customer**. The only thing you can learn when you talk is how little you know. Although there are plenty of situations when you want to be speaking to help educate the customer or share information with them, speaking less and listening more is a good guideline. Many excellent conversationalists only talk about 30% of the time.

2. **Listen Very Hard.** If you are not speaking, then you should be listening very carefully. This action is so necessary that I devote an entire chapter (Chapter 18 – The Listening Sales Engineer) to the topic. The key is that you need to listen to understand, not be listening to respond.

3. **Remember, It Is Not A Competition**. Just because your customer tells a story or a joke doesn't mean that you automatically have to tell one in return, especially if you try to one-up the person and tell an even better story. Do you want to leave the conversation feeling that you told the best story or that your client is happy?

CASE STUDY: JOHN AND TRAVEL

Over the years, I have learnt not to "one-up" my customers and tell multiple stories on top of their stories, except in one specific circumstance. I love to travel and am fortunate that running Mastering Technical Sales has taken me to many places and countries worldwide. When someone else starts telling stories about travel, cool places, and amazing sights, I just can't resist and feel I must contribute and share my stories. I like to think that I am sharing my world experience with others less fortunate, but that is not the case. It is a blind spot for me, multiplied by jetlag, and I have now adapted by not talking about my travels (unless asked) and always having another topic as an alternative. It still needs work. A lot of work!

We all have these blind spots – be cognizant of yours.

---

4. **Keep it Confidential**. Once you have gained the customer's trust, she may confide some personal or insider (politics) type information. When your customer invites you into their office and closes the door, it is usually a good sign. However, you cannot automatically assume that you are free to share that information with others on your sales team. If in doubt, ask your client. *"Would you mind if I shared that information about the new product plans with my account team?"*

5. **Use good judgement**. To state the obvious, you should stop the conversation if you feel that anything you are told is ethically, morally, or legally suspect. Ask, in your own culturally appropriate words, the equivalent of *"should you be telling me this?"*

The Five Factors

Credibility. No matter what type of conversation you are having, your credibility is still at risk. If you talk about a personal or professional topic that you know little about (in my case, subjects like ballet, basketball, or firewalls), just admit that it is not your strength. You can follow up with a statement about how you'd like to learn from everyone else in the room. Almost everyone wants to teach and be an expert! When speaking about an area in which you have significant knowledge, ensure you don't go into lecture mode. Take a breath and make sure everyone else is still breathing (and not sleeping).

Reliability. Much as in Credibility, your Reliability is still at stake, even in a more personal situation. Keep careful track of any promises, commitments, or even anything that sounds like a commitment. You need to get it done if you say you will do something, even as simple as sending a link to a funny YouTube video. Your Reliability is tested when your client introduces you to others within her organization. It is a modified form, but your client is relying on you to perform well and make them look good.

Intimacy. Non-deal-related conversations are one of the significant intimacy drivers, primarily when conducted in a neutral setting like a cafeteria, coffee shop, or restaurant. Although you can gain some personal and professional insights into your customer by observing their work surroundings (pictures, mementos, awards etc.), try moving the conversation away from a work location. Of course, that doesn't work for everyone, so you should consider it a guideline rather than a rule. Nevertheless, food and drink are universal catalysts for relationship building.

Self. Unless your customer is explicitly trying to find out as much information about you as they possibly can (and you then have to ask yourself why), aim for listening more than speaking. For example, answer a question, share some information, and then turn it back. (Using the travel example again...)

Customer: *John, have you ever been to Japan?*

John: *Yes. Several times and I have enjoyed every visit. Especially the hospitality of my hosts and the opportunity to learn a lot more about Japanese history, which is a topic of great interest to me. Please tell me about your travels to Japan? What did you like? (I could easily, and often do, talk about a topic like that for hours.)*

Positivity. One critical aspect of being a T/A is the ability and willingness to have a difficult conversation. You should remain positive even if discussing potentially changing personnel on a project, needing to make additional investments, or your client's stalled career. You may think they have already heard many of the proposed solutions. Yet you would be surprised how often that is not the case. Remember that a T/A should bring a blend of common sense and innovation to problems.

In Summary

Any conversation, business or personal or hybrid, with a client is an opportunity to improve your relationship. Mostly that happens through listening, asking the appropriate questions to further the conversation, and then listening again. Rarely will your client just expect you to lecture for 10-15 minutes, which is certainly to be avoided – unless they have given explicit permission for you to do that. Although you may expect more personal conversations to help your **S** and **I**, they can damage your **C** and **R** unless you pay the same level of attention to them.

Now complete your Red/Green worksheet for this topic.

THE TRUSTED SALES ENGINEER – Worksheet
Personal Improvement Thoughts & Tasks

Chapter / Topic	

Factor	Green List – Things To Keep Doing Well Or Even Better	Red List – Things to Stop Doing or That Need Big Improvements
Credibility		
Reliability		
Intimacy		
Self		
Positivity		

Table 10.1: Red-Green Improvement Sheet

Chapter 11: A Voyage Of Discovery

Discovery is not an event but a constant process. Although we Sales Engineers like to place Discovery early in the sales cycle (because it prevents big problems later), we should have the attitude that we are always in Discovery mode. That said, Discovery is the #1 place where there is friction between the SE and the salesperson. Many organizations rely on the salesperson to perform initial Discovery, uncover the business issues, and then brief the SE on what they discovered. The SE then takes this second-hand information, translates it into their product / services / solution set – and presents it back to the client. According to research data from the 4th Edition of MTS, around 40% of the time, this misses the target and ends up in a less than satisfactory customer interaction.

There has to be a better way, and it's not constantly *training the salesforce.* As a corporate portfolio grows deeper and broader, it is just as hard for the rep to keep up with the new requirements and marketing pitch as it is for the SE team to keep up technically. Your customer, of course, does not care about any of that.

Some General Discovery Guidelines.

1. **You Don't Have All The Answers**. That may sound counter-Credibility, but you really do not have to come up with all the answers in a Discovery call. Your fundamental job is to uncover all the customer issues (technical and business), listen carefully, and ensure you understand why they are issues. Do not engage in *Premature Solutioneering*.

2. **You Are There To Help.** Your attitude is that you are in the room or on the phone to help the customer – not to sell them something. Anytime you are explicitly selling or closing, you are anything but a Trusted Advisor. Turn ABC - Always Be Closing into Always Be Consultative.

3. **Beware Of The Easy Sale.** When your customer says, *"we need a reverse osmotic warp stabilizer,"* and that **is** what you are selling, it's easy to smile and count the commission. (That is what many reps would do.) However, you cannot just accept the customer's statement. You need to understand why they think they need your product. The 5% of the time you may lose a sale is balanced by the 25% of the time they need much more from your company.

4. **Look For Alternatives.** The second word in T/A is advisor. Many of your customers will be looking to you for alternative suggestions and ideas for tackling their problems. Be creative.

5. **Don't Over Emphasize The Pain.** Most sales methodologies talk about customer pain. It is a phrase I use in many workshops, yet it is not a good word to use with your customer. At least not until they use it first. Resist the temptation to get too "medical" and spend all your time diagnosing. Sometimes all you need to do is understand. And don't forget to seek out the Gains!

The Five Factors

Credibility. The largest enhancer of **C** during Discovery is asking the right questions in the correct manner. Your questions need to make sense to the client and provide a sense that you are making progress. Questions asked just to ask questions (or run through a routine checklist) are likely to slow things down. The instant your client thinks, *"why is she asking me that question?"* you will have Credibility issues. As in all sales situations, listening and then showing your understanding of the current (and future) state is vitally important. In most cases, the fact that the SE has a higher **C** rating with the customer than the account manager is an excellent reason for the SE to drive the Discovery session – both technically and on the business side.

CASE STUDY: AN ALTERNATE PERSPECTIVE

When I conduct Discovery with a client, usually a senior SE leader, one of my favorite questions is, *"if I were to ask your sales counterpart for their impressions of your team, what would they say?"* However, I've learnt that if I ask this question in the flow of the conversation, at least half the time, it brings everything to a halt as the SE leader wonders why I am asking that particular question and what I will do with the answer. So I now preface the question with a brief explanation like *"I'm going to ask a question so that I can get an alternate perspective on the situation – looking at things from a customer point of view. This proves to be extremely useful in fine-tuning our learning outcomes"*. The conversation then goes much better.

Reliability. During Discovery, R is more of a low-key factor. The initial customer interactions set you up to demonstrate **R** later when you need to follow up or take a course of action. However, if you have a history with the customer, there is the aspect of R in that they rely on you and your company to help them get something done.

Intimacy. Having warned you not to "go medical" earlier in the chapter, the **I** factor can be equated to your bedside manner. Yet again, this means covering not only the standard SE routines around speeds and feeds and metrics in general but also gaining an understanding of how your customer feels about the current state. Again, emotion plays just as big a part in the sale as logic.

CASE STUDY: THE PERSONAL TOUCH

Phil was a junior SE with a large infrastructure and tools software vendor. He didn't have much of a technical background but had extensive social sciences and psychology training. Once he understood the solution set (he said his company was a "glorified electronic plumbing unit"), his manager noted that he conducted some of the best Discovery meetings in the geography. Phil's secret was one magical question, phrased in a few different ways. He simply asked, *"How does that impact you personally?" or "What do you feel about that?"* His customers would open up and tell him. He quickly gained the Dr. Phil nickname, after the US television personality.

Self. This is not the sales cycle stage to talk about yourself or your company. Unless the customer specifically requests it because you have a Credibility gap. It's all about the customer, and using some of Phil's questions from the story above is an effective way to proceed when blended in with the technical questions we need to answer. There can also be a tendency to direct the conversation towards your strengths. Although you should cover those areas, it rarely hurts to learn about other issues/problems/desires that the customer may have outside of your specific solution set. There have been many times when I have been able to introduce a customer to another vendor or another technology, which has yielded no material financial return to me – except for an increase in trust that invariably pays off later.

Positivity. An 80 % / 20 % mix of pain and gain drives most opportunities. I've never seen a true scientific analysis to back up that number, but it is supported by examining many sales pipelines. That is a 4:1 ratio of bad:good, which isn't the most positive frame of mind during Discovery sessions or any form of conversation. Although, as SEs, we are trained to look for issues and how to solve them, don't forget the gains and positive outcomes that may result from the sale or the relationship. The gains create a powerful emotional bond between your product set and the customer.

In Summary

Discovery is all about the customer. Most sales techniques, nine-block models, and process flowcharts teach you how to control the customer and the conversation. However, no customer wants to be controlled. Let the conversation go where the customer wants it to, and gently give it a nudge now and again. For the SE, this is the most critical part of the sales process as information gained early in the cycle inevitably saves you (re)work later.

Don't make the mistake of explicitly using Discovery to show how smart and knowledgeable you are. That will come out naturally by asking the right questions, suggesting a few ideas, and then listening.

Now complete your Red/Green worksheet for this topic.

Chapter 12: Presentations And Demonstrations

When you ask salespeople or end-user customers what SEs actually do, they'll often reply that they are the folks who perform the demo and pitch the product presentation. Personally, I feel that is a sad reflection on the profession as we do so much more. Yet those tasks are a fundamental responsibility for most SEs. Putting that philosophy aside for a moment, there are so many ways that a Trusted SE can utilize the "outbound" parts of the sales cycle (when you are speaking more than listening) to improve all of the factors of the Trust Equation. What better place is there for Trust to turn into Advice that is gratefully accepted?

Some General Presentation And Demonstration Guidelines.

1. **Create An Agenda**. Even if the salesperson has created a very high-level agenda, create one of your own that details precisely what you will show and why it is important to the customer. Again, a small degree of personalization makes a big difference.

2. **Make It Relevant**. An "Out Of The Box" or "Out Of The Cloud" demo or standard corporate presentation rarely hits the mark, even for small SMB-type clients. Unless you have an incredibly technical audience using a checklist to score your features (and we all know it happens), avoid the feature tour and instead focus on how your customer will actually use your portfolio. Fire up their imagination!

3. **Don't Forget That You Are The Expert**. Show the customer something new or different or offer an alternative solution to the obvious approach. Use your judgement and coordinate your strategy with the salesperson – but be the Subject Matter Expert.

4. **Link The Technology Back To The Business**. I use the phrase "The Three Wonderful Measures + Mission," which relates to Increasing Revenue, Decreasing Costs, Mitigating Risk, and Satisfying Mission. Other people talk about People, Money, and Time. Technology alone won't build trust and won't get you the sale unless you link it back to the business drivers.

5. **Less Is More**. Just because you have 90 minutes doesn't mean you have to use it all or pack as much material as you can into the time. Instead, focus on what is essential and make it memorable. That's the reason why there are only six items on this list.

6. **Trusted Advisors Don't Over Use PowerPoint**. See the next chapter on Visual Selling!

The Five Factors

Credibility. The demo/presentation stage is a great opportunity for you to demonstrate your credibility and subtly present your credentials. Bad puns aside, this is the time when you are center stage and have the chance to shine. You are the master of your own technology, so it is essential to effectively link that technology back to the customer's situation and hopes, needs, and desires. The better you can help the customer walk into the future and envision how they can utilize your products and services, the higher your credibility. It proves that you have listened, taken the time to internalize some examples, and then personalized your work.

Taking the opposite approach, the customers feel ignored if you inject nothing from Discovery into your demonstrations and presentations. They think their time was wasted, which is not the way to gain trust. Your credibility plummets.

CASE STUDY: "WHAT WE WANT"

A few years ago, we ran a workshop with a mixed audience of Solution Architects and Account Executives from a large telecommunications provider. Their goal was to start the process of becoming a T/A to their larger clients, with whom they were conducting a lot of transactional business without much longer-term strategy or relationship building. As part of our discovery process, which involves sitting in on their client meetings and interviewing them, we noticed a few things that were getting in the way. Most noticeable was a mandatory "product update" session they ran every 3-4 months. The orders from senior management were that whenever the company released a new product or service, every client had to receive a presentation on it within 60 days. We label this the "Beauty Contest" or "Shiny New Toy" syndrome. It did not matter if the client needed a new service or even wanted to hear about it – the sales team gave them the presentation anyway! This was a massive waste of everyone's time, certainly did not show that they were actively listening, and resulted in steadily declining incremental revenue.

As part of many operational and cultural changes proposed over the next six months, they made the update optional at the discretion of the sales team in conjunction with the customer. In the next quarter, only 44% of the customers received the "product update," yet 75% subsequently purchased it. As a result, revenue on that line item increased fourfold.

Reliability. Thinking of **R** as Do As You Say, this sales cycle stage highlights the implicit promise or bargain you make with the customer during Discovery. What is the bargain? It is that you will provide "the perfect solution" in return for the customer's investment of time, people, and even money earlier in the cycle. That is the promise you make. If you don't deliver on that promise and slant your pitch towards what you want to show instead of what the customer needs to see, all your trust factors will decrease, especially **R**. Ignore the customer and pay the price. No one wants to feel they are given a repeatable, reused, second-hand off-the-shelf pitch even if they ask for it!

Intimacy. One major piece of advice is that when you say "we," – it should mean your company and the customer in partnership. Not "we" as in "my company" or "we can provide'. If appropriate, this is also the time to link some of the items you are showing or present back to those softer "Dr. Phil" questions from Discovery. This action completes the personal gains loop for the client.

Self. You ought to show some "Professional Self" and be proud of your company, your solution, and even the way you are communicating. Just ensure you are on the proud and confident side of the emotional scales and not on the arrogant, most brilliant person-in-the-room side. It is OK to say "I" when expressing your opinion or telling a story but do not overuse the word, or it becomes overbearing. The alternate view is that you bury your ego and personality in total favor of the customer and be excessively humble. I don't feel this is true to yourself, but it can be very effective with some presenters. Recommended action is to be yourself.

Positivity. In most demonstration situations, confidence equates to positivity. Do not take it to mean saying Yes to every customer (or salesperson) question and request. In fact, that would have a detrimental effect on your **C**. No product can be that great and that perfect a fit. Instead, improve both **C and P** by the judicious use of customer anecdotes to illustrate a point. Remember that the answer to *"can your product perform <capability X>?"* isn't always *"let me show you that feature."* Sometimes it is a Yes or a No followed by a brief customer story about how someone else uses <capability X>.

CASE STUDY: WHOEVER TELLS THE BEST STORY WINS

A standard part of New Hire training is presenting a new SE with a comprehensive case study. Many companies now do this as part of the actual hiring process. The SE then has a set time to develop a demo or presentation that matches the case study's facts. It is a learning opportunity plus a chance to put the new SE under some real-world stress. One of the typical questions from a sales manager is to wait until the SE shows some complex screen, take note of an esoteric feature / option / checkbox and then wait five minutes. Once the poor SE was now 3-4 screens or slides further on, she would ask a question about that little-known feature. The actual test, both in the case study and in real customer situations, is whether the SE goes back to show that feature, asks a question about how the customer would use it, or stays on their current screen and relates how another customer uses it. The last two options are great; the first one will doom you to a life of speeds and feeds. Mid and senior-level customers will delegate you downwards to people who sound as technical as you. Building up trust from the bottom rungs of the ladder is hard work.

In Summary

If presentations and demos are a key responsibility of your position, then take the opportunity to make them professional, relevant, and even entertaining. You will be ahead of the game by showing the customer the possible successful outcomes from using your product and then linking those back to the business drivers and the requirements.

Middle management and executives in the room will appreciate not being overwhelmed with technical features. In contrast, the individual contributors will appreciate you doing a great job in front of their boss and their boss's boss. Especially if they are the ones who got you the initial invite into the room!

Now complete your Red/Green worksheet for this topic.

Chapter 13: White Boards and Visual Selling

"I See What You Mean!"

I believe there is a direct link between the willingness and capability to use a whiteboard and your perception as a T/A. Forget about some of the "trained monkey" programs that companies roll out where they teach their sales force a canned value proposition board and then expect them to deliver it verbatim. They just don't work and have a lifespan of a few months. I'm speaking about a form of visual selling you can personalize and customize for the client. There is so much Credibility to gain when you sketch something for the client. Because it is an idea or concept that goes straight from your brain via your hand to the physical or electronic board. It is personal and your concept, not some PowerPoint that a Product Marketing person in HQ has built for general use.

Some General White Board Guidelines.

1. **Bring Your Tools.** Every SE should carry their own set of marker pens: four colors – black, blue, red, and green plus a four-color pen. Consider them an essential part of your hi-technology toolkit. (Travel advice – if you go through airport security with too many pens (>20), they will stop you and search your carry-on bag.)

2. **Bring Your Tools - Part 2.** You will need a fine point stylus if you use an eWhiteBoard. No one over ten should be allowed to draw

anything with a mouse or finger. Don't forget a spare AAAA battery if using an active pen.

3. **Start Simply.** Using a visual approach encourages simplicity. Your message will be messy and confusing if you try to pack too much onto a canvas surface.

4. **Collaboration Is Awesome.** Encourage your customer to add, delete, modify, and interact with your drawing. If you are doing this electronically, give them their own pen to encourage collaboration.

5. **Ask Permission.** Always ask your customer's permission before you start drawing. *"I thought we could sketch an example of the overall architecture if that's OK with you?"* In 30 years, I have never had anyone tell me, *"No. Use PowerPoint or Google Slides instead!"* Yet the common courtesy of making the request, especially in Asia-Pacific countries, is immense.

6. **Use Your Creativity.** Draw on the back of a napkin or a sheet of paper ripped off a pad. If you are in a conference room with no whiteboard in sight, ask if you can draw on the windows instead. Technical audiences love it. One of my SEs (Richard, you know who you are) once turned around a US $1.5m deal with a quick sketch on the glass window of a Wall Street data center.

CASE STUDY – NO, NO .. DON'T ERASE IT!

As an Information technology executive, I had to sit through my share of boring vendor presentations and executive bonding sessions because a vendor wanted to become my trusted business partner. The best sales calls were those that didn't feel like a sales call because they left the laptop in the car. One call, in particular, was with a sales-SE team who, for 45 minutes, showed me how they could redesign my network and implement a far more robust backup strategy for my IT organization. The sketch we collaborated upon ended up on the

---

whiteboard in my office, and I left it there (with their name on it) for almost three months.

I must have walked the entire executive team through that diagram and validated it with my technical team in the process of securing unbudgeted funding to get the deal done. Of course, this vendor team displayed many other good sales habits, but they certainly confirmed their T/A status with me throughout the six months. To the point that they could get an appointment almost on demand, I'd act as a reference for them and ask their opinion about other IT purchases entirely unrelated to their portfolio.

The Five Factors

Credibility. As mentioned above, the fact that you are willing to take a little risk and draw your solution or idea or even facilitate a meeting does wonders for your credibility. The downside is that you have to know your material, as you don't have a bunch of bullet points on a slide to use as a presentation crutch. However, the upside is that you gain the flexibility to adapt to the client and collaborate to work with them instead of presenting to them. As a starting point, practice being able to design and deliver your own personalized 6-8 minute vignette pitch on many topics. A good choice would be a big picture, overall value proposition, architecture overview, and a diagram/explanation of some competitive differentiators.

Reliability. One of the more advanced characteristics of Reliability is anticipation. Be prepared for questions the customer may have, and anticipate a "what-if" solution to a new problem. You can whiteboard almost anything if you know your solution well enough and have sufficient customer examples. Remember that nothing you draw will hang in the Louvre or Tate Gallery; it just has to be good enough to get your point across so the customer can remember and understand it.

Intimacy. One part of intimacy is to communicate in the easiest manner for the customer – to put them at ease and make them naturally more receptive to your thoughts. According to the Visual Teaching Alliance[23],

---

[23] http://visualteachingalliance.com/ , accessed 20 June, 2015

65% of the population are visual learners, so it is a method to personalize and customize for your client. In a small setting (such as 1:1 or 1:2), visualization is a great way to pull your client out of a formal office environment and have a conversation in the cafeteria or a coffee shop. In an even larger group setting (like 1:3 to 1:8), you can still get everyone engaged at a board and eliminate the email distraction.

Self. As with any other communication mechanism, you need to be aware of the difference between a presentation and a conversation. Let your audience agree with, modify, and even redraw part of the sketch. This format encourages collaboration and buy-in because a joint diagram becomes a common solution, which is a massive psychological step forward. When I want to promote collaboration, I put spare markers on the table for the audience to use or give my client their own pen if I'm in a 1-on-1 situation. It is about empowerment.

CASE STUDY: LET'S RUN IT UP THE FLAG AND SEE WHO SALUTES IT

Frank is an SE for a large enterprise software company and is part of a group that sells to the US Federal Government. His account is part of the military side of the Department of Defense. Some sales are direct to the end user military units, and others are made through various Systems Integrators. The common feature is that no sale is ever quick, easy, or closed without bureaucratic interference. Frank had an army background and, over a 15-month engagement, had cultivated the trust of the Brigadier General who headed the selection committee. At the end of yet another presentation, the one-star general asked Frank to stay behind for a few minutes. He handed Frank a leather-bound notebook and said, *"Frank, draw me a picture of how it will work that I can use to explain to other non-technical staff."* Breaking the military rule of "Be Bright, Be Brief, and Be Gone," Frank took 30 minutes to walk him through the process, teach him how to explain it and make sure he understood all the implications of the project. Two months later, Frank's company completed a multi-million procurement process. Not to make it sound like too much of a Hollywood ending, but Frank was also promoted, got a nice bonus, and was invited to Sales President's Club.

Positivity. I have a natural and positive (no pun intended) bias towards visual selling as it promotes solution design and collaboratively solving problems. It is a genuinely positive activity, yet it must be carried out professionally. So my usual question is, *"would you be willing to sign your name on the bottom of the diagram?"* If you are willing to autograph it, it is good enough (remember it's not going to hang in an art gallery); if it isn't, you need to go back and practice a bit more.

CASE STUDY: USING THE MAC-NAPKIN

In the late '80s and early '90s, I worked for Oracle as their first presales engineering manager in the newly formed vertical group, when they were a $100-200m company. We had a sizable deal pending with Eli Lilly, the pharmaceutical company. So we needed to win over their R&D drug development group during a corporate visit to the old Oracle HQ in Belmont, CA. I took half my team out for the visit as we had some complex demos and proof points to show.

One of my roles was to brief the speakers and presenters at the visit about Eli Lilly and the objectives of the meeting. Almost everyone on the schedule wanted a quick 5-minute brief and then returned to their busy jobs. Except for two people. The first was Larry Ellison, who spent 30 minutes with my VP. The second was a fresh-faced rosy-cheeked Product Marketing Manager named Marc Benioff – who was responsible for Oracle on the PC and MAC platforms. Marc and I spent nearly an hour in the company cafeteria, using a healthy supply of Oracle*Napkins, outlining how the Lilly R&D team could use their Macs as a front-end to all the corporate data they had stored on VAX, UNIX, and IBM systems. He came into the meeting two days later and, using a chalkboard (it was a long time ago), absolutely nailed it. My team of David Lesniak and Mark Shiner then produced one of the all-time magical demos that concluded with a distributed SQL query across six platforms from a PC front-end. Deal done!

I always thought that Benioff kid would go far in life.

In Summary

People who are uncertain about its applicability raise many objections to whiteboarding. You must overcome your fear of poor handwriting, of short silences while you draw, of being "on the spot" with no bullet points to guide you, and of artistic ability. On the plus side, it is a real differentiator if you invest in the skill.

Over my career, I have white boarded in front of luminaries like Larry Ellison, Mark Hurd, Tom Siebel, multiple CIOs and CEOs across the world, obnoxious Wall Street Managing Directors, and characters ranging from stoic Chinese Government Officials to a quiet Japanese Board of Directors to a group of wild Australian IT Guys in shorts and t-shirts. It works. It is personal. Drawing build Trust.

Now complete your Red/Green worksheet for this topic.

Chapter 14: Handling Objections and Giving Answers

Sales Representatives handle objections, and Sales Engineers answer questions. It is a subtle distinction, yet it takes some contentious elements out of a Q&A session and can turn it into more of a conversation. Many "objections" that classic sales theory tell you how to "handle" are just questions. By a non-scientific study of listening in to thousands of sales calls, I'd confidently say that about 85% of classic objections are simple questions posed because someone wants to know the answer. There is no malice, evil intent, or laying of landmines behind the question – your customer just wants an answer!

Some General Q&A Guidelines.

1. **Start With Yes And / Or No.** Make life easy for your client! If possible, start your response with a clear Yes or No. Don't turn your answer upside down to do it, especially if there are two, four, or fifty shades of grey in your response.

2. **Make Sure You Understand What Is Being Asked (And Why).** Just because you are, or wish to become, a T/A, doesn't mean that you should be over-eager in answering every question straight away. When you are in a situation and don't understand why a question is being posed or the motive behind it, it's OK to ask. As usual, frame your response in that better clarification will help you to give a clearer and more precise response. You'd be surprised what you can learn.

3. **Balance Completeness Against TMI (Too Much Information).** There is a delicate balance between telling the customer what they need to know and telling them everything. TMI can make your answer sound rambling and unfocused. It can also get you into trouble by accidentally revealing something the client doesn't need to know. Trusted Advisor doesn't mean full transparency, 100% disclosure over everything! Most married couples aren't that good.

4. **Provide Examples**. For responses with some complexity, look to provide concrete examples so the client can internalize your answer. That can be as simple as "*in your environment that would mean..*" or talking about "*your data centers in Adelaide and Beijing*" instead of "*data centers A and B.*" Usually, the concrete answer is better than the abstract response.

5. **Get Affirmation or Buy-In.** The only way to know that you answered the question to the customer's satisfaction is to ask them. Not after every question, but certainly after the critical questions. Remember that a "Yes" can mean "No" in some countries.

6. **Great Question!** Don't say that[24]. It implies not all the other questions were so great.

The Five Factors

Credibility. Experienced SEs pride themselves on the ability to answer every single question asked about their product. Many consider it a badge of honour. It certainly can drive up your C rating if you handle whatever the individuals, managers, and executives might throw at you. Yet there is something a little disconcerting about someone with all the answers. That pride can turn to arrogance or even the "*smartest person in the room*" syndrome. It is not your job to prove how smart and knowledgeable you are. It is your job to help the customer. So approach a Q&A session with

---

[24] For more listen to Dave Stachowiak of Coaching For Leaders: https://coachingforleaders.com/podcast/thats-a-great-question/

that intent, rather than wanting to score 100% and return serve with winners. I was once advised, *"John, Sales Engineers are NOT paid by the word."* **Think about that.**

CASE STUDY: WATCH THE BODY LANGAUGE

Early in my career, one of the salespeople I worked with videotaped a joint seminar session we gave to an audience of several hundred people. She told me it was a training video for others in the company who would provide the same seminar the following month. She also used it to prove a non-verbal point with me as she felt I was too aggressive in handling questions. I, of course, totally disagreed with her. Reviewing the video - my entire stance and demeanor would change whenever I was asked a question. As the question was being asked, I would widen my stance, crouch down an inch or two, put my hands in front of me – and generally look like I was physically ready to tackle the person asking the question.

I was playing a win-lose sports game instead of a win-win relationship game. Lesson learnt.

Reliability. This factor takes a backseat in most of the Q&A process. There are R aspects in terms of your customer contact potentially relying on you to make a good impression on his team or with his boss. The concept of reliance on your technical and business acumen shines through in the interaction. In general, Q&A type interactions are mostly neutral for your R score.

Intimacy. Much of the I score is carried by the non-verbal aspects of the communication. That means looking at the person who is asking the question, acknowledging them by name if possible, demonstrating that you are listening, and then carefully maintaining some eye contact when responding. The obvious inference is that physical Q&A sessions can be more productive than virtual ones (unless they have already met you and established some trust). Also, using the customer's personal and corporate language will make your response resonate even better. (Note: I have an irritating personal habit of unconsciously imitating distinctive accents – don't go that far to blend into the environment). Finally, when conducting virtual Q&A, you should have your camera/video turned on to humanize yourself and encourage your customer to do the same.

Self. My personal story shows that I was making the Q&A session about me and not about the customer. My primary concern was not letting the figurative objection ball get past me, which came out loud and clear during the session. You can also consider engaging other customer experts in the conversation, if safe and appropriate, to allow them to demonstrate their expertise. We underestimate the art of facilitation when handling questions.

Positivity. It is also a requirement for the SE to put their answer in a positive but realistic light. If there is a problem or an issue, then that needs to be acknowledged and dealt with to the customer's satisfaction. Accepting an issue or a strong emotion is a major requirement of being a T/A. Note that acceptance doesn't necessarily mean agreement, especially if someone is upset, but you can certainly understand why they feel the way they do.

In Summary

Answering questions is a wonderful way for an SE to display their talents and capabilities subtly and understatedly. Rather than have a customer leave the room saying, *"wow – that SE knows her product,"* you may be better off, from a trust point of view, having them feel confident about you and your solution and lowering their perceived risk of taking action. You certainly don't want to show that you are the most intelligent person in the room – just someone who can help the customer get to where they need to be to fix their business problems. It's a humble attitude.

Now complete your Red/Green worksheet for this topic.

Chapter 15: Strategic Accounts vs. Small Medium Business

At this point, some of you may be thinking, *"this is all wonderful for the larger strategic accounts, but... I work with SMB (Small Medium Business) accounts. How does it apply when you only speak with your customer a few times?"* The short answer is that most of the preceding and following chapters apply with a modified approach. This chapter will cover how you become, in effect, a Trusted Advisor to your territory and the individuals within it.

Here is a beautiful story explaining why small clients are just as important as larger ones.

CASE STUDY: FROM SMALL ACORNS, MIGHTY OAKS CAN GROW

"As a junior SE in the mid-90s, I helped sell a small system to a small manufacturing company in Southern Germany. My primary contact was Krystal, the IT systems administrator. All I remember about the deal was a lunch a few days after the contract was signed when I gave her some advice about system setup and how to reduce her support payments by a few thousand Deutschmarks (it was that long ago!) a year.

Twenty years later, as a senior VP, I entered a conference room for what we feared would be an extremely complicated meeting with a challenging but potentially valuable client. Krystal was in the room as the CTO and main decision-maker. She remembered me, thanked me for my help and kindness twenty years previously, and then started the meeting. During one very contentious discussion, she just looked at me and said, "Max, will this work for us?" I replied that it would, and we averted another two hours of unpleasantness. A few months later, our newest customer was delighted with our solution, we had a fantastic reference, and I had a newly established executive relationship."

Some General Smaller Account Guidelines.

1. **One More Time.** Always go into every meeting, assuming you will see the customer again. Of course, you want that encounter to be pleasant and professional. Never do or say anything (or allow anyone else to act in that manner) that you may regret later.

2. **Decisions Aren't Always Faster.** You may think smaller companies have fewer people involved in a decision so that they will act faster[25]. Not always the case because they can be more risk-averse.

3. **Risk Is Even More Important.** A mistake such as data loss or delayed implementation may be an inconvenience (and recoverable) for a large company - it can put a small company out of business.

4. **An Executive Is Still An Executive.** It doesn't matter if they are the CxO of a 50, 500, or 50,000-person company. They will still care about money, time, and people.

5. **Small Businesses Talk To One Another.** Communications between small businesses in a specific territory or industry are more extensive than those of larger companies. The amount of networking and vendor reference checking at the monthly business meet-and-greet in the small town I live in amazes me. These companies readily talk to their competitors, as their common enemy is the large multi-national corporation.

---

[25] https://www.challengerinc.com/sales The CEB says there are now between 6-11 stakeholders involved in most technology decisions in larger corporations.

6. **Trust Will Get You Access To Power**. Quickly! SMB Companies are used to dealing with many vendors for just 1-2 meetings, and then they disappear. Differentiate yourself, and you have a fast route to the executive boardroom.

The Five Factors

Time scales are sometimes shorter for the smaller accounts, meaning you must be on your best behaviour throughout the sales cycle. That includes not just the meetings but also email, voicemail, and any other forms of interaction you may have with the customer.

Credibility. Your credibility is key with these accounts. You may well recommend the optimal configuration of your solution and, potentially, an implementation plan. Although the customer may have an in-house expert, they will still rely on your technical and business capabilities. In these situations, your job is to quickly help the client narrow down a list of options and arrive at the correct outcome. Being able to cite other clients and supply plenty of comfort and reassurance will ease the path to this outcome. If you get something wrong, make an answer up, or otherwise "fake it," you have a minimal chance for redemption. So "*I don't know*" is an acceptable answer, as is "*I'm 98% sure we handle that, so I'll confirm it as soon as we finish this meeting*". You can also gain considerable **C** by informing the customer what problems they don't have. That kind of reassurance can be very comforting to a small business. As a final thought - participating in local events such as User Group meetings is a fantastic way to boost your **C** rating with a large group of users.

Reliability. Reliability equates to rapid and complete follow-up. SMB deals have their cadence and timing. Every salesperson will tell you there is a perfect window to close a deal, and if you miss that window because a technical question is unanswered, the deal will push to a later close or even disappear. A Major Account SE may have 8-12 active opportunities in a quarter, whilst an SMB SE can have over 50. You cannot afford to let things slip or delay responses, so your time management and the time management of others are critical.

CASE STUDY: YOU NEED TIME FOR TIME MANAGEMENT

"For a short period, I was responsible for a group of inside Sales Engineers. Their sole responsibility was to assist the inside sales team in qualifying larger deals or rapidly closing smaller ones. They spent most of their day on the phone or Zoom / Meet, doing remote web-based demos and presentations. It was a brutal, unrelenting schedule, and we had significant employee satisfaction issues and turnover. Looking at schedules, I noticed an incredible number of back-to-back sales calls and even calls scheduled during lunch because of time zones. The SEs barely had time for a bathroom break, never mind follow-up. In fact, they conducted most follow-ups after the close of business or before calls started the following day.

    As an experiment, we set defined call times for the SEs in 50-minute blocks with 40-minute follow-up periods (for example, 08:30-09:20, then 10:00 until 10:50). This resulted in 6 possible daily calls, with built-in recovery/follow up time between the calls. Over the next six months, morale increased, attrition was almost down to zero, and our closure rate increased by 10%. This was mainly because we conducted follow-up immediately after the call while it was still fresh in the SE's mind rather than relying on notes ½ day later. The power of being reliable."

    Steve, SE Director Inside Sales & Channels

Intimacy. The I score is the hardest to boost with SMB clients because of the transient nature of the interactions. This dictates working on what doctors call their "bedside manner." Interestingly, in these days of relatively brief doctor-patient interactions, there are multiple sessions at many medical conferences devoted to this subject. It is a common problem. Some easy steps are to use the customer's name, know a little about their company before speaking with them, look for similarities (maybe you use their products), and avoid technical jargon. Sharing something about yourself, either verbally or on an intro slide, can often help to improve your I score. As for Credibility, participating in User Groups and relevant Trade Shows can also boost the I factor.

Self. As in many other situations, listening comes to the fore when faced with just a few interactions to make an impact. Reverting to the medical example, studies show that physicians stop the conversation and redirect the patient after about 20 seconds, while patients need 32 seconds to complete their explanation of concerns. A famous medical quote by Dr. William Osler (founding father of Johns Hopkins Hospital in the US) states, *"listen to the patient; he is telling you his disease."* Our equivalent is *"listen to your customer; he is telling you his problem"*! Silence is OK. If your customer pauses in the middle of a sentence or an explanation, don't jump in to fill the silence. Allow a couple of seconds to pass, and focus intensely on your customer to prove you are still listening.

Positivity. Given the limited number of interactions you have with an SMB type client, it is unusual for the Positivity score to vary much from the default of 1.0. Since we've been using many medical examples in this chapter, the old physician's creed of *doing no harm* applies – providing a balance of reassurance and practicality.

CASE STUDY: SHUT UP AND LISTEN

At Mastering Technical Sales, we use Constant Contact[26] to handle our email lists and distribute newsletters. It may not be the cheapest solution, but it works effectively with a minimal amount of our time and is well worth the monthly fee. A salesperson for a rival company caught me at my desk, and I foolishly picked up the phone. After explaining *"who we are and what we do,"* he asked about our current situation. Always eager to view other small business sales habits, I explained our situation to the rep just in case he could help us. I don't think I managed to get more than 3-4 sentences together before the rep interrupted me to make some unhelpful point about his services (like "we can do that too"). It totally wrecked the flow of the call, and after ten minutes of the back and forth, I challenged him on this technique as he'd spoken more than 50% of the time when asking me questions. It was all about his email/list services, not my company. We agreed to stop the call. He even interrupted me when I thanked him for the information he provided. Sigh. S=5

---

[26] http://www.constantcontact.com

In Summary

The primary behaviour to remember from this chapter is always to go into every SMB meeting with the assumption that you will see the customer one more time and treat them with professionalism and respect. Timeframes and interactions are certainly limited – and in practice, you may never map out a T-Score plan for a small account, yet the fundamental guiding principles of raising trust will still apply. Small customers talk to each other, and their staff moves as often as larger customers do – so having a reputation as a trustworthy individual within your geography or vertical is a great long-term play that pays dividends the longer you are in that territory. That is true even if you work at another company selling in the same market.

Now complete your Red Green worksheet for this topic.

Chapter 16: A Trusted Advisor To Sales

Sales Engineers have many customers. They are not just the customers who sign contracts and give us revenue. The SE organization also has Sales as a customer and often external Partners. The world's most incredible SE is rendered ineffective when not trusted by Sales. No one will collaborate with that SE and take them on calls, preferring to use other SEs. Therefore, a salesperson must trust their SE and vice-versa. You need to establish confidence that you not only know the technical capabilities of your solution set but also that you can "handle yourself" in a sales situation and not say or do the wrong thing.

Some General SE And Sales Trust Guidelines.

1. **With Not For.** SEs work with their sales counterparts, not <u>for</u> them. Being subservient doesn't establish much trust – or at least not the right kind of respectful trust.

2. **Respect The Boundaries**. Asking the rep to reforecast and requalify the deal may not go over too well. If you don't have enough information, ask questions but avoid sounding like a Sales Manager or an RVP at a Quarterly Business Review. Sometimes a simple smile and "playing dumb" can work wonders.

3. **Be The Expert**. Be confident in your technical capabilities <u>and</u> business acumen. You are the Subject Matter Expert in the room – act like it without acting like the smartest person in the room.

4. **Ask for Advice**. As previously mentioned, it's very rare for a salesperson to resist the temptation of teaching an SE about sales. People love to teach. Even the lone wolf rep at 160% of quota wants to explain how she does it.

5. **Think Big**. Look for ways to expand the deal. That may be by adding more products, services, or new users to a project. The T/A Sales Engineer can grow the deal faster than anyone else in the salesforce. If your sales process involves The Challenger Sale, this is a high potential area for you.

6. **Be Positive**. SEs are taught to look (proactively) for problems in a deal and raise them to the attention of sales and their SE management. Look for positives about the deal so that they can be emphasized and reinforced. Provide balance.

CASE STUDY: THE PARKING LOT EXPLOSION

"My first sales call with Jim was eventful. He was a strong and powerful rep who liked to "front-run" technical questions by providing a partial answer before handing it over to his SE. As one of the few female SEs in the company, I was used to being treated well by the customer and not so well by some of my older male colleagues. During the demo, Jim started to answer every single customer question. That frustrated everyone. After five or six of these interruptions, I began to jump in before Jim or assert myself by standing or moving to a whiteboard. It didn't go down that well with him. The call ended with meeting our goals and getting the customer's agreement to add another product option. Nevertheless, we barely made it out the front door before Jim turned to me and started to complain bitterly about my behavior.

I stood my ground and responded that I would never dream of answering questions about pricing, legal, or contracts (even though I knew the answer). I expected him to stay out of what was clearly my turf – and we'd negotiate the middle ground. It took a few more calls to get to a steady state and then a few more calls for Jim to start specifically requesting me as his SE. Game over!"

- Cheryl, Chicago, USA.

The Five Factors

There are a couple of general points to make that cross many of the factors. The first is that most salespeople love to be *sold*. A logical, stick-to-the-process approach that may seem natural to an SE may not appeal to a run-n-gun ad-hoc salesperson. You often need to mix a lot of emotion into the discussion to convince the rep that it is in their interest to listen to you and then potentially take your advice. The second is that, ultimately, the accountability for getting the deal lies with the salesperson and not with you. If you have never experienced the pain of sitting in a sales meeting and de-committing a deal or lowering your forecast, it is not a pleasant experience. Therefore, although the following commentary on the factors is SE-slanted, never forget who is fired if the number is consistently missed. It is not always the fault of sales, but they ultimately pay the price!

Credibility. Many salespeople associate high **C** directly with technical competency and the capability to communicate that competency to the customer. As we learnt in Chapter 5 - those are skills #4 and #5 from a customer viewpoint. Although that reversal of the skill list may seem a little puzzling, look at it from the salesperson's point of view. It is their job to understand the business, ask the business discovery questions and build the relationships – they don't necessarily want you to focus on that. They need someone to support them once the technical bits, bytes, and features start flying through the air. Your value is linking that technology back to the customer's business requirements. When you give a rep a super-tech SE, I can guarantee that within a few weeks, SE management will hear a complaint about *"They're great technically, but don't have a clue about the business or how to speak with management."* So – depending on your job role, start with technical competency as the basis of your sales C score, and then rapidly demonstrate the other business or solution-oriented characteristics.

Reliability. Another frequent complaint of salespeople is that "their SE" doesn't follow up appropriately or only follows up under direction and supervision. There is no excuse for this behaviour. If you miss a deadline, then it is your issue. Either you didn't work hard enough, or the deadline was not realistic, and you didn't renegotiate the timeline.

CASE STUDY: "A" OR "B"?

"Kim was one of a half-dozen inside reps that my group supported. She was notorious for making promises to the customer and then dropping them on the SE team as absolute commitments. As a result, our group engaged in *heroic efforts* that satisfied Kim but stressed out the team and resulted in an unfortunate resignation. Management did not care as Kim was hitting her numbers. On my next interaction with her, she presented me with two conflicting assignments. I could get one completed, but not both. The conversation went like this.

Me: "Kim, I can complete "A" or "B" by 5 pm today, but not both."

Kim: "You need to get both done; I promised the customer."

Me: "Only one. You choose which is more important, "A" or "B" – they are both your accounts."

Kim: "You need to get both done; I promised the customer."

Me: "Only one. You choose, and then contact the other customer and tell them we'll have it done by tomorrow afternoon."

Kim: "I promised."

Me: "Sorry about that. Next time, why not add 24 hours to your delivery date? That way, we have flextime and can still complete ahead of time and beat expectations. Have you ever lost a deal because you responded in 24 hours instead of 8?"

Kim: "Well, no, but I'm going to escalate this to your manager."

Me: "That's not a great way to build this relationship. Before you go have that conversation – which project should I start on, "A" or "B"?

Kim: "B."

Chak, Singapore

As well as taking care of the apparent follow-ups on time, being proactive is a great way to demonstrate Reliability. Once you have agreed on the standard rules with the rep and then the steps before and after a sales call – look for an opportunity to follow up with the customer without being specifically told what to do. <u>Your inbox should not dictate your actions</u>. Even if you are a young SE in an RFP factory environment, you still have opportunities to get in front of the tasks instead of reacting to them.

Intimacy. This is the most critical factor in the sales-presales relationship and often the one most neglected. Getting to know your sales counterparts and what motivates them (contrary to popular opinion, it is not always money) is critical to the relationship and the steady building of trust. Since most SEs have a reputation for being techno-geeks, coming across as a regular person who just happens to excel with technology can be a major benefit. Since most salespeople are social people, and we are generalizing here, you can accomplish a lot by sharing just a little about yourself. Add in asking for help or advice, particularly how to build a relationship with a new client or deal with an awkward personality, and the I score can increase rapidly.

Self. Handling **S** with your sales partner is quite different from that of a regular customer. With a customer, you may be aiming for a score of S=1. For a rep, I'd suggest that S=2 is the goal. **Setting S= 1 with a rep can be self-defeating.** Even within the best sales-presales relationship, there is still considerable tension, especially in the areas of adequate discovery and the velocity of the deal. If you put the best interest of the rep at heart, you are, in effect diminishing yourself in the relationship, as the rep will tend to take advantage of you putting them first. Think about it! You still need some sense of identity and self-determination to stand up for what you believe in, do the right thing, conform to a sales process, and help the customer. So – yes, you are working towards a common goal of a happy and satisfied customer. However, your definition, the salesperson's definition, and how you jointly get there may be different.

Positivity. As mentioned in a few other chapters, no salesperson wants to be surrounded by negativity and told why the deal wouldn't happen. Bias your attitude towards the positive, tempered with reality. We often accuse reps of having "happy ears" and only hearing and interpreting words from the customer that lead to a deal. Your job is certainly to encourage that viewpoint and seek out the positives, balanced with anticipating issues to overcome. Pitching this to the sales side of the house as *"preparation and planning"* is better than *"the competition will kill us with that new feature."*

The other side of the P factor is keeping a positive outward attitude in front of the customer (even when all others are panicking). The best explanation of this is from Rudyard Kipling's short poem "If-"[27] which is one of the best job descriptions ever!

In Summary

So many SEs focus on becoming a Trusted Advisor to their customers that they forget about the salespeople they work with daily. Winning and keeping the trust of one salesperson has a cumulative knock-on effect on the other members of the sales tribe. Once you have one rep in your corner who fully trusts you, others will follow, and it becomes much more manageable. Listen hard, ask for advice, and respect the boundaries – as long as both sides agree. If there is no agreement, **S** and **I** will suffer, and the relationship will be in conflict, which inevitably shows up in front of the customer – if only in body language and attitude.

Sales are as much a customer of the SE as the end-user, revenue-producing customer is – and building trust is essential with both if you wish to be a genuinely successful SE (and ultimately an SE leader).

Now fill out your Red Green worksheet on this topic. You know you can improve your relationship with that one troublesome, difficult rep!

---

[27] Rudyard Kipling , If- http://www.poetryfoundation.org/poem/175772

Chapter 17: The Social Sales Engineer

(This is the first of three final "how-to" chapters in this section and focuses on the S and the I with your customers – so the format is slightly different.)

G rowing up in England, I learnt very early on in my life (thanks to my Auntie May) that great things can be accomplished and many problems can be solved over a cup of tea. The same principle applies to the business of being an SE – you can build a relationship with a bit of food and drink[28]. I've probably agreed on as many deals in a local coffee shop as in a formal meeting – from Stockholm to Singapore to Sydney. In a sign of global brand ubiquity, Starbucks in the Singapore OCBC building, and the nearby Boomerang Bar, have been particularly successful meeting places for Mastering Technical Sales.

Making A Start

Do not think that "entertainment" is something only the salesperson can and should do. If you are a field-based SE, especially when you travel, anytime you eat alone,[29]you are wasting both networking and relationship-building opportunities. It is surprising what clients will share with you once you get them out of the office setting – it is better than having them close the office door. The company cafeteria can be better than a meeting room or a cubicle. Even Public Sector clients (who may not be allowed to accept anything from you) loosen up outside the building. The key to any social meeting is that it becomes a conversation. Giving the client a sales pitch with the laptop in the local tearoom is not your goal.

---

[28] I'm editing this in May 2020 as Covid-19 runs rampant in the expectation that things will return to relative normalcy at some point in 2021.

[29] Never Eat Alone, Keith Ferrazzi and Tahl Raz, Random House June 2014.

Think of conversation, not presentation, as a mechanism to increase your "I."

HINT: I'M IN THE AREA

One of my favorite approaches was contacting a customer (or a prospect) and telling them, "*I'll be in your area next Monday, and can I drop by for a few minutes?*" *Of course,* I'd always state that I was by myself (which translates as "no salesperson with me") and would love to catch up with them over a tea/coffee/beer – whatever works for them. The success rate of getting a "yes" was terrific.

BONUS HINT: DON'T ALWAYS MEET WITH THE SAME PEOPLE

Ask, "*is there anyone else you'd like to invite or think I should meet?*" You may worry about not getting 1-on-1 time with your primary contact, but if they have something important to share, they will find a way to share it with you.

An important part of the Trust Factor is to let the conversation go ahead at its own natural pace. Rushing into the "business" part of the conversation is a mistake. You may need to give a nudge here and there to the overall direction, but do not force it; otherwise, you are showing a high "S." On Wall Street, it may take less than a minute to move past the personal; in Sydney, it could take a couple of beers, whilst in Tokyo, you may never get there in a first meeting. Remember, whenever the customer speaks, you have an opportunity to learn something about them.

The Inside Sales Engineer

If you are an inside SE, do not give up hope, as alternatives are still open to you. Think about any of the following:

- ✓ Do you have any customers within a 25-mile (40km) radius you can meet out of the office?
- ✓ Do you ever travel for training or internal meetings?
- ✓ Can you volunteer for trade show/booth duty?

✓ Are there customers you know well enough that you can schedule a solo catch-up call?
✓ Can you make it a video call instead?
✓ Do you know any field SEs who might let you tag along on one of their meet-and-greet sessions?
✓ Ask your boss for help.

EDITORIAL NOTE: No. The salesperson does not "own" the account. Your company owns the account and lends it to both the rep and the extended sales team (that is, you) in return for revenue and customer satisfaction. So ask forgiveness instead of permission. Go meet a customer.

Don't Tie It To Revenue

Resist the temptation to pair your meetings with potential short-term revenue. That is an obvious ploy. It will damage both your C and your S with the customer. If the first time you call a technical contact with an offer of coffee is 4-6 weeks before a forecasted deal is to close, everyone understands the motive. However, the reality is that you <u>are</u> in the business of helping sales to close their deals, so choose potential transactions that are 6-12 months out if you want to be selective. That way, your intent to "sell them something" is far enough in the future that it will not show in your verbal or non-verbal communications.

Stating The Obvious

Just for the record:

o Be on time.
o You offer to pay first. (Subject to local and government customs)
o Clean up after yourself.
o If you make commitments, summarize them at the end of the meeting.
o Thank the customer for their time – and mean it!
o Follow-up with a thank-you within 24 hours.
o Suggest you repeat this in 3-6 months, so it is not a one-time thing.

The Ugly Downside

You will leave the meeting not only with some helpful information but also with a list of items affectionately known as **CYJs – C**an **Y**ou **J**usts? These might be following up on open support tickets and getting answers to technical and sales-related licensing questions. They are the price you pay during the relationship-building phase, as you must give something to get something in return. CYJs can prove to be a cheap and rapid way to increase your R factor – but they are extra work.

In Summary

Do not spend your time hiding behind electronics and your inbox as you waste three good daily opportunities to improve a customer relationship. Even if you can't meet with a customer, try meeting with one of the sales representatives (and not to speak about a specific deal), someone from an overlay team, product management, support, or maybe a services person who is in the office that day. The power of developing a personal relationship that is not explicitly tied to something you want **right now** will power up your T-Score!

Complete the Red Green worksheet for this topic with your social engagements and profile in mind. Then, however large your social network is today, set a goal to expand it by a fixed percentage over the next 90 days.

Chapter 18: The Listening Sales Engineer

"What am I going to say when this idiot finishes talking?"

*(This is the second "how-to" chapter in this section and again focuses on the **S** and the **I** with your customers – so the format is slightly different.)*

Knowing when to speak and listen is the most critical skill of a Trusted Advisor Sales Engineer. Add to that the understanding that when you are not sure if you should be speaking or you should be listening – you should be listening! Get that wrong, and you will be in the position of advising without trust, and no one will listen to you. Now layer on top of that the fact that it is not good enough just to listen. You actually have to demonstrate that <u>you are listening</u> and make the customer feel like you are paying attention.

This is not an easy skill to acquire or maintain, yet it is essential (in any culture) to becoming a top-class Sales Engineer and a Trusted Advisor. Sadly, many SE organizations invest so much time in practicing their outbound skills around demonstrations and presentations that they neglect their inbound talents around listening and confirmation.

Active Listening

What is the role and usage of Active Listening for the Sales Engineer? First, we will start with a definition and the distinction between hearing and listening. **Hearing** is the process of sound waves leaving the customer and entering your eardrums. It is the acknowledgment of noise (or silence) and nothing else. For example, you might say, *"Can you hear that?"* adjusting the volume on your speakerphone, or my wife will say, *"did you hear that?"* when a floorboard creaks late at night in our house.

Listening implies an active process within your brain once the sound waves hit your eardrums. For example, if the CEO of your company speaks directly to you, I would bet that you are listening to her rather than just hearing her talk!

The second part of the definition distinguishes between different styles of listening.

A. **Vacant Listening**. Have you ever had a conversation with someone and known they are not listening to you? They may be on the end of a phone doing their email or physically in the same room as you (possibly even uttering encouraging "uh-huh" and "ok" phrases), yet you are 100% certain that they could not repeat a word you have said? That is Vacant or *"Sorry I was distracted; can you repeat that?"* style Listening.

B. **Self-Oriented Listening**. Although the other person is both hearing you and listening to you, the only reason they are doing so is to promote their point of view instead of thinking about yours. The big clue here is that as soon as you finish speaking (or even before), the other person jumps into the break to either counter your statement or one-up it. We have all been in that situation of meeting that person who always has a better/funnier story to tell than yours. I characterize this as *"what will I say when this idiot finishes talking?"* listening. Sales Engineers fall into this category when they at once diagnose a customer's problem early in a Discovery meeting and interrupt the customer to tell them about their great solution!

C. **Passive Listening**. The listener is actively listening and understanding you yet provides no reflective or indicative signals that they are in this behavior mode. Think about speaking to someone for five minutes by phone, yet they never utter a sound – how do you know they are listening? Maybe they are asleep or doing email?

D. **Active Listening**. This occurs when you are genuinely interested in what the speaker is saying, how they are saying it, and attempting to understand how they feel about it. This involves not only listening but also confirming in various verbal and non-verbal ways that you are both listening and understanding.

So How Does This Apply To A Trusted Advisor Sales Engineer?

As a practical application, let us focus on a Discovery meeting – where you should listen far more than speak. So here are a dozen tips for you to consider and practice – and always remember Rule Zero:

The only thing you can learn when presenting to your customer is how little you know about them.

1. **Stop Talking**! It's hard to be an active listener when your mouth is moving. Without significant training, our brains cannot handle speaking and listening concurrently (think simultaneous translators!)

2. **Provide non-verbal signals** to emphasize that you are listening. This would include nodding/wobbling your head, making eye contact, and making hand gestures. Lean slightly towards the speaker and keep your posture open (do not cross your legs away from them, for example). When facing men, face them squarely and women at a slight angle. Perform all the gestures and nodding, even if operating remotely via a webcast, as they affirm your mental intent, which is communicated non-verbally. Taking notes also counts as a non-verbal signal –do not overdo the notes to the point that you lose track of the conversation!

3. **Provide verbal signals** to encourage conversational flow. Think of these as brief, positive verbal prompts. English examples would be *"OK," "I understand," "And?"*, and *"Then what happened?"*

4. **Be Patient**. Not everyone processes information or explains events the same way you do. Give the customer time to make their point in full before you jump in. An extra moment of silence often yields

a valuable nugget of information. The exception to this tip is when one of you communicates in a non-native language and needs help with the "right" word.

5. **Show Empathy.** When a customer is talking about a difficult personal or professional situation, take a few seconds to look at it from their viewpoint. You can follow up with a statement such as *"how did that make you feel"* or *"what do you think the business users thought about that?"*

6. **Restatements**: Using your judgment, restate or paraphrase what the customer has said. (Note I do not say repeat, or parrot, their words). You can lead into this with phrases like *"just so I'm clear on this"* or *"let me confirm I'm getting this."* Use this technique to prove to the customer that you are listening and remove any doubts from your mind. You can also try mirroring, which is repeating the last few words or phrases the customer has spoken.

7. **Summarize**. During a natural pause in the conversation, or if the customer has covered much ground/discussed many issues, take the opportunity to summarize. For example, *"so it sounds like to me that you are concerned about three things, and those are .."*

8. **Don't Rush To Judgment**. You may be able to diagnose the customer's problems within 5 minutes as you have seen those problems many times before. This is their first occurrence for the customer, and they need time to explain and process them. You are probably right – but interrupting after 5 minutes doesn't make you look smart. You'll give the impression of arrogance instead. Be patient – you may be wrong, and you may learn something useful in the time it takes the customer to feel they have fully explained themselves.

9. **Resist the DAC!** Step away from the temptation to *Disagree, Argue or Criticize* until you have collected all the facts and emotions from the customer. Even then, you may want to show some patience. Once you dive into the **DAC,** your listening mode will revert to Self-Oriented instead of Active.

10. **Probe**. When you sense there may be more to an issue or customer statement, try using a probing question once the customer has finished their statement. Examples would be *"who else is typically impacted when?"* or *"what do you think will happen if this problem re-occurs?"*

11. **Don't Be Defensive.** Sometimes it is difficult to sit there and hear the customer out when they are attacking you, your company, or are (in your opinion) completely wrong. Just remember that the more information you have about how they feel, the better you will be able to handle the situation. My wife always tells me, *"stop being such a guy – you don't always need to rush in and fix things; sometimes, all you need to do is listen."* Wise advice indeed!

12. **Follow-Up**. Sixty minutes of effective active listening is destroyed by a lack of follow-up. So if you have promised or committed to any action items – get them done As Soon As Possible. It also helps to send back a summary of key points from the conversation (but not in all countries – be careful) to ensure that you did "get it."

Relating Back To the Trust Equation

Active listening will improve every factor in the equation.

$$T = \left[\frac{C+R+I}{S}\right] P$$

Credibility will improve as the customer feels you are not rushing to judgement but are weighing the facts. **Reliability** increases as you have an opportunity to show an understanding of the conversation and act upon it. **Intimacy** improves as you start to move towards how the customer feels. **Positivity** increases as you work together to create a positive outcome for a business problem. **Self-Orientation** decreases as the focus is not on you but the customer. The not-so-simple act of listening can have a significant impact on your "T" scores.

In Summary

What happens when you do not listen? There is a birthday party game trick of lining up 10-12 children in a row. You whisper a message to the first in line, who whispers it to the second, and so on. The message that comes out of the mouth of child #12 is vastly different from the original. The anecdotal military story tells of a World War I British army officer who signaled *'send reinforcements, we are going to advance,'* which was converted into *'send three and four pence, we are going to a dance.'*

SE organizations spend hours and hours perfecting demonstrations, fine-tuning slides, planning installations, and building impressive ROIs. Yet unless you collect the correct information, it is all a futile exercise. So listen, listen actively and listen hard!

Complete your Red Green sheet for this topic, looking at situations where you can (a) prove you are listening and (b) improve your listening.

Chapter 19: The Culturally Aware Sales Engineer

(This is the third "how-to" chapter in this section and focuses on all the factors related to cultural and geographical differences in trust – so the format is a little different.)

There are obviously many cultural implications around the development of trust and the giving and receiving of advice as you travel worldwide. It is fair to say that although trust is essential no matter where you are, how you obtain it and then utilize it is a different matter. To put that into perspective, it wouldn't be unusual for a 30-year-old Sales Engineer to sit down with a 50-year-old customer executive or vice president and have a conversation as (almost) equals. Or would it? You would certainly expect that in the US, most of Europe, and Australia. It would, however, be very unusual in Malaysia, Japan, China, and even some parts of Europe, such as France or Belgium.

In many societies characterized by a high **power distance (P-D)** number[30], power and authority are basic facts of personal and professional life. Not everyone is equal, and everyone has their rightful place and level in life. Leaders resolve disputes without much input from their subordinates and expect 100% compliance with their tactical instructions and strategic directions. What seems strange and inefficient to one culture is natural and highly productive in another.

So how does a Sales Engineer operate as a Trusted Advisor in this situation? Access to higher levels within your customer will be restricted based on rank and authority. It will be extremely awkward to have a "difficult conversation" with a customer, especially in a group setting. You

---

[30] For more on this review the works of Geert Hofstede : http://geert-hofstede.com/ : Geert Hofstede, Gert Jan Hofstede, Michael Minkov, Cultures and Organizations: Software of the Mind. Revised 3rd Edition. New York: McGraw-Hill USA, 2010

will also need to overemphasize the importance of the customer in the relationship and make sure they always look good. There are issues going "the other way" when you are used to high power-distance and have to work in a low power-distance country. You may not be used to speaking with people 2-3 levels above you in the hierarchy, speaking your mind, and honestly challenging the customer.

Although this chapter is written for SEs in low P-D cultures moving to high ones, there are words of advice when making the reverse move.

Some General Cross-Cultural Guidelines: (From Low To High)

These are some guidelines if you come from a low power distance culture (say the US or Scandinavia) and are now dealing with a medium to high power distance organization, person, or culture (such as India or Japan)

1. **It's Going To Take Longer Than You Think**. Relationships drive everything, and it's going to take longer to build each factor. Getting down to business before the connection is fully formed will limit your T score. The easiest way to think of it is that you are starting from a default position of *"don't trust"* instead of *"do trust."*[31] The relationship, once made, is incredibly durable, so you must spend the time on a solid foundation. You need patience, which is not always the strongest character trait of "go-getter" alpha western males.

2. **You Are Being Constantly Observed**. Imagine that the customer is writing a report card on you for every meeting. Then they submit that report card to the executive level within your customers.

3. **Dress For The Part**. To paraphrase an older piece of career advice, *"dress for the meeting you want to have next, not for the one you are now in."* That does not mean you must outdress the salesperson, wear a Rolex, etc. It does mean being neat,

---

[31] That's not the case, although serves as a good analogy

presentable, and highly professional – even in a virtual setting. Also, observe the status symbols around your customers. Use compliments.

4. **Utilize Circles Of Influence**. Your intended Trusted Advisor target may be out of reach, particularly if they are more than a single hierarchical level above you. Instead, you may need to become a Trusted Advisor to an internal advisor of that customer. Developing a relationship with someone in close contact with a senior executive is often like speaking directly with that executive. Plus, if you provide enough value, you may eventually be sponsored for that meeting. It will (see point #1) – take time.

5. **Trust ≠ Value**. Trust is not generated by the initial value you bring but is often driven by that common relationship (a party member, children at the same school, community, or a longtime business relationship). As a result, an SE may need to operate through a proxy connection for a very long time.

CASE STUDY – THE THREE-HOUR DINNER

In 2011, a colleague and I met with "KC," a potential customer, for dinner at an extremely nice restaurant in Hong Kong. We had a significant enablement proposal in front of this customer, as he was the decision maker and budget holder. The proposal made a lot of economic and business sense for him. My colleague, the sponsor of the meeting and all the initial conversations with KC's staff, was far more aware of the cultural aspects than I was. To summarize an hour of the briefing, he said, *"He has read your book and likes your philosophy of what it means to be an SE. Don't talk about the proposal unless he does first, and give him a signed copy of the book as a gift at the end of dinner no matter what happens."*

A multiple-course dinner took three hours, and we spoke about everything except the proposal and his team. On many occasions, I barely resisted the temptation to pivot to business. However, I resisted it (with great effort!) and put my "get to the point" attitude to one side. At the end of dinner, we said our goodbyes. I presented him with the book, he gave me a small gift – and we parted ways. I thought that although it was a pleasant three hours, I had made no progress.

My colleague called me early the following day – absolutely ecstatic. He had spoken with KC's administrative assistant and learned it had been an *extraordinary meeting* and that we would have the contract signed within a week. I was stunned, amazed, and then happy. Lessons learned were many. I had listened to one of my Trusted Advisors, implemented their advice against my not-so-better judgement, and learnt a lot about business in that part of the world.

Some More General Cross-Cultural Guidelines: (From High To Low)

These are some guidelines if you come from a medium to high power distance culture (say Malaysia or Japan) and are now dealing with a low power distance organization, person, or culture (such as the US, Israel, or the Netherlands).

1. **Prepare For Surprises.** You can be introduced to a senior-level executive when just walking down the corridor – or have the CEO sitting next to you in the cafeteria (there are no separate executive dining rooms in most low P-D cultures!). So be prepared to have a conversation – and it may not be about business.

2. **Expect To Be Asked For Your Opinion.** You have an opinion that may not match the room's consensus. Be prepared to express a contrary point of view (and have the facts to stand behind it) or agree with the majority (and say why). Many managers seek everyone's opinion and aim for consensus rather than making a definitive decision. Listen for words like "feedback" and "buy-in."

3. **Time Is Money.** It's entirely possible you may exchange pleasantries and small talk for just a minute and then get right down to business. It's not rudeness; the perception of the

monetary value of time and a person's calendar drives the behaviour.

4. **It's OK To Say "No."** This may be the most challenging aspect of the low/high (or high/low) conversion – using the word "no." Although many cultures are reluctant to say "no," it is permissible in many situations. When asked to do something clearly impossible, costly, or unethical, you can obviously say 'no". You can also say 'no" in many other situations if you have an alternative proposal.

The Five Factors

Credibility. Credibility comes in two forms. First, there is direct credibility in terms of your product, business, consultative knowledge, and how you express it. Then there is indirect or reflected credibility regarding your qualifications, plus what other people think and say about you. Leverage referrals and contacts, and do not overly self-promote yourself.

Reliability. Reliability does not change much from culture to culture. You still need to commit to your words (and often your word is your bond) and under promise, so you can then over-deliver. You must also consider consistency regarding your reactions, responses, and general behaviors. The crazy erratic "techie" is not always as highly valued as they might be in a Silicon Valley startup.

Intimacy. Building a relationship can take much longer and must be done in a methodical, systematic process. You cannot rush and shortcut the system. You will also (see "S") have to give your customer plenty of credit, "face," and honor in front of others. Do not expect much other than polite recognition until the T scores start to elevate. Do your research and understand the importance of age, position, business cards, chopsticks, greetings, and all the other cultural traps just waiting to trip you up.

Self-Orientation. Bury your ego for the sake of the relationship and the greater good of the two companies, and avoid imposing your cultural expectations on others. Do not totally submit to *"the way things are* *done*." Your customer is speaking to you and interested in a relationship for a reason, so you are supplying value. Invariably part of that value lies in the fact that you are an outsider.

Positivity. I've heard this referred to as humble or quiet confidence and can't think of a better way to describe it. Rather than repeatedly showing an overly positive attitude, let your body language do the work instead of your mouth. Look and act confident, be prepared to reassure your customer in times of trouble, and utilize your network or circle of influence to amplify that confidence.

CASE STUDY – BROKEN IN BAHRAIN

Most of my personal stories deal with successes, but this story deals with an abject failure of how one culture expresses trust compared to another. I had been speaking with Michael, who ran the Middle-East SE organization for a large petroleum and mining engineering company. After several conversations with Michael, we had come to a verbal agreement on a few remote sessions and a couple of videos that his media team would translate or subtitle. Being a good old-fashioned presales guy, I wrote up our agreement as a set of notes and action items and then sent it to Michael for confirmation before we proceeded to contract. I received a very curt and brief response in return.

Fast forward a few weeks, I discovered that I had offended Michael by writing our verbal agreement (his operations chief used the word "Westernizing") as Michael felt he had already agreed to everything. One lost deal. Over the next 4-5 days, I discovered multiple stories and case studies of people making the same mistake as I did. Again – numerous lessons were learned. First, that trust is expressed and stated differently, and second, my research/discovery was horrible. I should have known better.

THE TRUSTED ADVISOR SALES ENGINEER

And The Workaround

When stuck in an unpleasant cultural situation, you can always fall back on your own culture: "if we were in <your local culture>, I'd certainly act differently. However, I recognize that is not the case, so help me out here; what would you recommend?" The fallback of asking for advice can be a good one and is usually not interpreted as a sign of weakness in this situation (unless you are negotiating a major contract).

In Summary

Operating as a Trusted Advisor in a country outside your own is both a challenge and a valuable learning experience. In one case, you need to be far more subtle and indirect in your approach, while the exact opposite is true in another. You need to prepare for different levels of access and different timelines to gain trust. You will also find far more faith in networks of friends, colleagues, and families in many cultures, and the classic "friend of a friend" approach can serve you well. The most effective approach is to be consistently respectful. This respect extends to dress, to let someone start a handshake/touch first, body language, hierarchy, and to the roles of sexes. Taking a stance of humility and learning rather than one of certainty and preaching goes an exceptionally long way.

Yet to finish as I started the chapter, it's fair to say that trust is important no matter where you work. However, how you obtain it and then utilize it is a totally different matter.

Complete the Red Green worksheet looking for situations where you can learn more about another culture or just improve what you are doing within your own culture/country.

Section 3: Getting There From Here

"Love all, trust a few, do wrong to none."

William Shakespeare (All's Well That Ends Well)

The final section looks at how to put it all into practice. The organizational change to move an entire sales group towards a T/A attitude is immense, so the easiest starting place is with YOU. I say this because most readers are either individual contributor Sales Engineers, or first-line SE managers. You can personally achieve only a certain amount of change. What you do have control over are your attitude and your actions. Like any sales opportunity, executive sponsorship is crucial in closing the deal, but NOT starting it. In our case, the deal is a real commitment to a T/A program, not just lip service.

There are several Bonus Chapters at the end of this section. They contain additional material from the classes and some of the research data. Please complete the short self-survey and assessment at the end of Chapter 25 and feel free to send it to me via the website. Also, try out the *"What Would You Do?"* Case Studies in Chapter 27.

Chapter 20: Current State: Where Are You Now?

I t's highly likely that although you are willing and able, the current state is a random collection of negativity because of:

o   Confusion over how to become a Trusted Advisor.
o   Staff turnover within the sales (and presales) ranks.
o   A strong monthly or quarterly pressure to "hit the number'.
o   A transaction versus relationship bias in sales planning.

Those important behaviors are rarely measured and rewarded despite what it may say in your corporate vision or mission statement. Although a few companies pay a form of bonus based upon customer satisfaction, that is not a measure of the relationship. It is a measure of satisfaction – which can be quite different. It is possible to be very satisfied based on a series of simple transactions without forming any trust at all. For example – I am delighted with the papergirl who delivers my Wall Street Journal every morning. Other than some reliability, as I know the paper will always be there – there is no formation of a T/A relationship.

Let's start with some fundamental questions and actions to determine the current state.

1.   **Make A List**. Review your current accounts (active in the pipeline and passive with no activity) and list your key contacts. Rather than go through a complete T-score analysis with each of them, categorize them as High/Medium/Low on the Trust Scale. You are looking for those accounts and key contacts where you already

have a fair degree of trust built up. That is the optimal place to start when you decide to take action.

2. **Do You Do Some Of This Already**? Realistically, everyone embodies part of a T/A in their client relationships. Is this behavior conscious or subconscious, and what are your strengths? Based on what you have read to date and the worksheets you may already have completed – which of the five factors can you lead with (and which needs the most work?)

3. **Does Your Company Do Any Of This Already**? Are there any corporate-sponsored programs or initiatives that you can utilize? Look for anything that deals with relationships, CSAT/NPS scores, feedback programs, or even customer advisory boards. You may also find sales sponsored programs around customer retention, breaking into a new market/vertical, or a new major/strategic accounts program. Any of those may have utility in gathering data about the current state.

4. **Is This Something You Really Want To Do**? Again – you start with you, then expand to your immediate group/division and ultimately to the company. It will be arduous work, and there will be many obstacles in your way, so you'll need a reserve of determination and a good deal of planning to overcome those obstacles.

5. **Is There Someone You Can Team Up With**? If you decide to start the T/A journey as a team, you already have a support mechanism. However, if you are beginning solo, you will need someone to partner with (as two are better than one) or at least someone to mentor you.

You Keep Saying Start With You – What Does That Mean?

Since you are half of every one-on-one relationship, you need to understand exactly what motivates you and how others perceive your personality and style. One of the simplest places to start is with one of the standard personality profile tests. These include the long-established Myers-Briggs[32] test, the DiSC[33] behavioural profile, and more complex options such as Strengthfinders[34] . They each have their inherent strengths and weaknesses, yet for sales types situations, the simplicity of the DiSC model is adequate.

To quote directly from the EPIC / DiSC profile website[35]:

"DiSC measures your personality and behavioral style. It does not measure intelligence, aptitude, mental health, or values. DiSC profiles describe human behavior in various situations. For example, the DiSC questionnaire asks about how you respond to challenges, how you influence others, how you respond to rules and procedures, and about your preferred pace of activity."

The DiSC model discusses four reference points:

Dominance –   *direct, strong-willed, and forceful*

Influence –   *sociable, talkative, and lively*

Steadiness –   *gentle, accommodating, and soft-hearted*

Conscientiousness –   *private, analytical, and logical*

Because I prefer colours, which reflect your style rather than abstract letters, I translate the characteristics into four primary colours[36]. Think of the mapping as shown in Tables 20.1a and 20.1b

---

[32] MBTI : http://www.myersbriggs.org/my-mbti-personality-type/mbti-basics/
[33] DISC : https://www.discprofile.com/
[34] Strength Finders 2.0 : http://strengths.gallup.com/110440/About-StrengthsFinder-20.aspx
[35] https://www.discprofile.com/what-is-disc/how-disc-works/
[36] https://www.insights.com/ There are companies that make a living doing this for you.

D	Red	On Fire, Always in Hurry. Time is Money.
I	Yellow	Bright and Cheerful (like the Sun). Social and mostly Extravert.
S	Green	Like the Earth. Concerned about the Big Picture and happiness of others.
C	Blue	Cold (although not really). Process and Rules and Logic driven.

Table 20.1a Colour Mappings

D	Dominance	**Achieves success by taking decisive actions towards their goals.**
I	Influence.	**Achieves success by persuading others to work with them towards the goal.**
S	Steadiness.	**Works with others as part of a team to achieve success.**
C	Conscientious.	**Works within rules and procedures to achieve success.**

Table 20.1b: John's Translation of DiSC to Colours.

The DiSC results will show you how best to work with others and take account of and utilize those differences. So read the results carefully and review your blind spots as much as you do your strengths.

For example, I am relatively **Yellow** (social) with a solid **Red** stripe (getting things done) which I need to run a workshop and drive my various projects to completion. I have some **Green**, as my mission is certainly to help the profession of the Sales Engineer. I have almost no **Blue** whatsoever – except when it comes to making my travel arrangements when I am a total *#traveldiva*!

It's also highly likely that you may have a different persona at work compared to your home life and exhibit other traits under stress (known as "back-up behavior").

Characteristic	Description	Relevance to John
D Dominant RED	Achieves success by taking decisive actions towards their goals. Time is money	Don't be short and sharp with John unless he is in a hurry or just needs a Yes/No answer
I Influencer YELLOW	Achieves success by persuading others to work with them towards the goal. Social and talkative	Take time to have a conversation and ask about his family, his business and his travels
S Steadiness GREEN	Works with others as part of a team to achieve success. Interested in the greater good	He has an interest in mentoring and improving the profession of the Sales Engineer
C Conscientious BLUE	Works within rules and procedures to achieve success. Data driven	Unless it is a contract or his travel arrangements – don't overload him with data

Table 20.2: Utilizing The Colour Schemes When Dealing With John

CASE STUDY: DETAILS, DETAILS …

Allan is one of my customers out in the Asia-Pacific area. The first time I dealt with him in putting a set of workshops together, he constantly asked for more details. My standard proposals and outlines were not exactly at the War and Peace detail level, so I relied on verbal walkthroughs in addition to the limited printed material. Allan asked for full timelines of the classes, samples of the slides, details of learning outcomes, and a lot of other material I had to create specifically for him. At first, I found this mildly irritating (having almost no Blue myself), but then I realized that as a Yellow/Red dealing with a Blue, I needed to provide this level of detail. Why didn't he trust me to deliver as promised? It was not a matter of trust; it was providing what was needed to make the client satisfied and comfortable with our capabilities. I could have let my ego run away with the situation; instead, I (eventually) saw an opportunity for improvement.

That was many years ago. Allan and his company have become one of our regular customers, and we have jointly produced many successful engagements for his SE team and expanded into multiple regions. Yet I must still review every session in detail (although not as much as the first time) with Allan –

because that is how he works. I also gained some great templates and outcomes that I now include as part of a standard proposal in an appendix – just in case I have any other bright Blue clients.

Understand Your Values

What is it that you genuinely believe in – both personally and professionally? Those values and the belief system drive your behaviour. Try writing those beliefs down on paper. You will find they are like the initial definitions of Trusted Advisor in the first few chapters of this book. You will know them when you see them – but the initial definitions can be challenging.

Many years ago, when working at Clarify, we held a workshop with The Pacific Institute[37] during an SE Leadership offsite. This organization focuses on self-improvement, visualization, and true "know yourself" seminars. I struggled with an exercise about values, and the facilitator said, *"John, imagine someone is speaking at your funeral – what would you want them to say in your eulogy?"* My first thought about that unpleasant subject was, *"Surprise! He's not really dead."* Then I got into the spirit of the exercise and discovered it did help me understand more about my values and personal brand.

You can start with the simple items about family, always willing to lend a hand, a sports coach, upright and honest, offbeat sense of humour, and so on. Then move into more specific items like "always treated others with fairness and respect," "promoted women in engineering," etc.

Mini-Exercise # 20.1 – Your Values

Try it. Then ask a few of your friends what they would say your values are. You may not want to bring up the funeral topic with them.

- ✓ Kind to children and animals
- ✓ Sports coach
- ✓ Supportive friend

---

[37] http://www.thepacificinstitute.com/

✓ Weird sense of humour
✓ Would always make time for you
✓ Willing to try almost anything at least once

Mini Exercise # 20.2 - Get Some Feedback

360-degree feedback was all the rage in Human Resource circles a few years ago. It has uses for the Trusted Advisor as well. In addition to the "eulogy/values" exercise in the preceding section, try running a T-Score analysis with the following individuals:

1. Your boss.
2. Your skip-level boss (someone two levels above you).
3. Several of your peers.
4. Several of the salespeople.

Once you have the T-Scores completed, take a leap of trust, and review them with these individuals. You may have to miss the 2-levels-above boss, but everyone else should be very approachable. See how their feelings about the relationship match yours and note any significant disparities between the views. This means that you need to be very honest in determining the status of the relationship, and if you don't feel that you can share the information, that tells you something about the current state right there!

In Summary

Start with yourself! Although you should certainly investigate and utilize any efforts and initiatives that your company may be undertaking – the only person who can position you to become a Trusted Advisor with your clients is you. So you understand your strengths and weaknesses and how you appear to others. It is not always a pleasant exercise, and I've learned a few things about myself over the years that I've either ignored or denied until confronted by someone willing to have that conversation. So seek them out, understand your motivations (so focus on the S and the I), and adapt accordingly before you commence your T/A operations.

Chapter 21: Future State: Setting The Vision

Now we are going to walk into the future. Just as you might with a customer during a sales opportunity. It is crucial that you understand the possibilities and at least set out some targets. We'll quickly touch on organizational change, review some short, medium- and long-term goals and start laying out some benefits. Much of this is company- and culture-specific, so think of this chapter as a highlights guide. You supply the operational details.

Organizational Change

The primary advice is to go first and lead or be one of the program's leaders. It doesn't matter what level you are in the organization; people will still watch what you do and how you behave more than what you say. *"You can't become a Trusted Advisor through PowerPoint"* was a great comment from one of our students. You must live the ideals of being a Trusted Advisor, so admit mistakes and quickly clean up after any errors. Take responsibility, and please avoid the blame game. Then, as the program starts to develop and the successes occur (and they will), you can celebrate those with a bit of pride. We talk more about that in Chapter 23 – What Could Go Wrong?

If you are in a position of some authority, accept that you cannot force a T/A program onto others. They are going to have to accept it and apply it for themselves. The rest of the team must become convinced that there is a better way to deal with customers and form long-term, mutually beneficial relationships. For example, we do not provide clients with a completed T-Score rubric or scoresheet. It is far more effective when they create it themselves, debate the details, and then fine-tune the numbers.

Setting Program Goals

Return to the start of the book and reread the Bottom Line Up Front introduction. Pay attention to the various metrics our client measured. You need to measure something to prove the program is working and that it is not just a *"feel good"* initiative. Unless you are rich in data and metrics, you may want to select just a few of the metrics that you consider to be:

1. Impactful – They make a difference to the business.
2. Measurable – You can realistically measure them without significant effort
3. Independent – Other events won't materially impact them.

The following three sections have sample short, medium, and long-term goals based on experiences with numerous clients. Each section holds some summary thoughts and recommendations. The speed of trust varies depending on many factors – but time is one of the steadiest and most reliable. Note that if your SE organization has a Presales Operations team, they may be able to assist you in gathering and examining some of this data – but most of it will initially fall upon you to accomplish.

Short Term (Less Than 9 months)

Remember that nothing will happen in the first few months.

1. General improvement in T-Scores for targeted client individuals. Set a goal for % or raw T-score gains.
2. Increase in referencibility[38] of targeted clients. (Set % growth or raw number increase)
3. Increase in the number of referenceable clients. (Set % growth or raw number increase)

---

[38] It is apparently not a word according to the dictionary. I am still going to use it.

4. Reduction in "time-wasting" calls and activities at target accounts.
5. Growth in the pipeline after month 6.

Medium Term (9-18 months)

1. All of the above continues.
2. Increase in Number of Active Revenue Opportunities per SE.
3. Increase in Leads Generated by YOU.
4. Increase in deal size (Average Selling Price) through meaningful cross and up-sell.
5. Decrease in random RFP and RFIs from target accounts.
6. Increase in "knock-on" (referral) deals. These are opportunities where one client may directly refer you to another department within their own company or to a brand new client.
7. You rarely eat alone or never at your desk.
8. Peers and others from outside the SE team seek your advice about being a T/A.

Longer Term (18+ Months)

1. All of the above continues.
2. Personal network is growing at a set percentage every month.
3. Ability to gain personal referrals and recommendations.
4. Invitation to attend (and contribute to) strategic planning meetings of the client.
5. Requests for advice outside of your company's primary market space.

In Summary

To reiterate one of the points above, you need to set achievable yet meaningful goals to prove this is more than some touchy-feely feel-good program. Be prepared for none of the measurement dials and needles to move for a few months, and change will only happen slowly and incrementally. Then if your experience is like many others, you will achieve a significant breakthrough with just one client, and everything else will fall into place as the success compounds itself and really starts to grow. Unless you have mounds of data to choose from, be careful in the number of metrics you select to watch. The more time you spend measuring, the less time you have to work on being the T/A.

Chapter 22: Bridging The Gap And Gaining Trust

The two previous chapters of this section examined some ways to determine where you are now and where you want to go with the T/A process. Having set up the base case, learning more about yourself, and then setting some achievable goals, it's time to start walking into the future and moving from the current state to the future state. Again, there is a lot of similarity between this T/A process and a sales process. One of the primary roles of an SE is to help a customer see how they could use your product/solution/service by building (or better yet helping the client to build) a path from now to then.

Based on *"every journey begins with a single step,"* plan out the first few steps to get you on your way. Here are three guidelines to help you along your travels. There is nothing special about these steps relating to being a T/A; they are simply reasonable project planning steps linked to a bit of personal psychology.

1. Play To Your Strengths
2. Make The First Steps Easy
3. Tie Those Steps to Your Goals.

The Pre-Work

To avoid assumptions, Table 22.1 shows the items you should have ready and in working order before taking the first major client-related steps. Again, you will notice that this is almost entirely about you and has very little to do with your customers.

Item	Description
T-Score Rubric	1-5 Ratings for CRIS And Your P Factors
Red/Green Sheets	Listing of Things You Do Well And Things You Don't
Chapter Sheets	Specific CRISP Actions From Section 2
DiSC	Your Own DiSC (or other behavioral analysis) Profile
Mentor	At Least One "Spiritual" Guide And Mentor
Goals	Short, Medium and Long-Term Goals

Table 22.1: Your Pre-work and Paperwork

Play To Your Strengths

We each have a Trusted Advisor profile – in that certain of the five factors are easier for us to achieve and later improve naturally. For example, most SEs are robust with Credibility and Reliability, neutral with Positivity, and struggle with Intimacy. Self is usually a positive trait but is most easily influenced by others with their own short-term gains. In other words, S is often the first attribute to crack under pressure. There is more detail on typical profiles in Chapter 25 – Your Trusted Advisor Profile.

You can approach the strengths in two ways. Firstly, you can seek to leverage your innate C and R factors as reasons to spend more time with your client. For example, if the time is productive and you have some measure of social skills, that will improve your I, S, and P scores. Secondly, if you already have some established S and I with a client, you can use that as a starting point to offer some service, time, or other "gift" that helps establish your C and R.

CASE STUDY: USING YOUR EXPERTISE

"Marc" (name changed at his request) is a virtualization guru. Barring a few dozen engineering people who work at VMware, he is the best of the best. In a humble way, he knows it – and his peers and the sales team he works with understand it. Marc would agree that he does not have the most engaging personality, yet he is one of those SEs that once you get to know him well enough, you are happy to spend more time with him. Marc's issue was that he was continually dropped into deals for a single meeting and never had time to form relationships with his clients.

His career mentor suggested that Marc focus on relationship building with just one person in every important meeting he attended, and find a way to follow up with that person, grab a cup of coffee, or otherwise engage with them. The barter for that engagement was access to Marc's tremendous expertise (i.e. his high C and low S in being willing to share). In return, Marc found opportunities to improve his R via follow-ups and his I through simple person-to-person interaction. He learnt that the *"how do you feel about that?"* question we promoted in earlier chapters worked wonders for him. Over the last decade, Marc has become a far more rounded Trusted Advisor (before it was all C driven) and has developed special access to the global executive suite with multiple CIOs and CTOs.

Make The First Steps Easy

Choose some targets within your customer base. Target sounds a little military, but as these are people you select and aim your attention towards, it works. Select at least six accessible individuals, ranging from almost total strangers to people you have known for at least a year. Half of them should be of a similar personality type as you are. For example, if you are Yellow-Blue, meaning quite social and outgoing, but with an eye for facts, figures and details – you need to seek out others who are anything but Red, with a good streak of Blue. To translate that: they will spend more than a few minutes with you without getting impatient and will care about facts and data! You will discover that you can gain a reasonable estimate of their primary and secondary colours after meeting someone for just a few minutes.

But why do this? It helps because you cannot modify your behaviour too much when dealing with these people – you can be your natural self. That leaves you free to focus on all aspects of becoming a T/A and improving the five factors rather than worrying too much about adapting to your customer.

Tie The Steps to Your Goals

Everything you do correlates with maintaining or increasing one of the T-score factors related to your specific client or your general behavior. As it will drive all the others, the primary goal you need to achieve is a measurable increase in your T-scores amongst your six selected targets. Note that you will also find that some other T-scores will improve by a point or two just because you are behaving differently – so don't be surprised to see further positive effects. Then tie those T-scores to an increase or decrease in something measurable. References, client/executive access, leads, customer satisfaction, Net Promoter Score statistics, and pipeline growth are all excellent places to start.

Once you have been going for a few months, integrate the T-scores into your Technical Account Planning. Organizational charts are the natural first place for inclusion. You will gain the added benefit of exposing others within the sales team to the T/A system if they're not already working with you on it.

CASE STUDY: CONVERSION RATE

A quick story from Sara in the UK. "We started a T/A program within our small part of presales engineering last year. Just three of us. After 8 weeks, we added a new metric to help us measure progress across the bridge you described. The metric was *conversion rate*. A convert was someone within our company who was interested enough in what we were doing that they asked for more information. Then they would check for an update, and finally, they'd ask what they could do to help or participate. After six months, we had at least one convert in every other important department within the company, then two, then three. The movement was gaining momentum."

In Summary

Increase your T-scores with clients who matter; everything else will eventually fall into line. Focus on the shorter-term goals; if those scores are moving in the right direction, you will be in a wonderful position to achieve those longer-term goals. Reassess progress every 30-45 days and look at the scoring graphically to spot any interesting trends. Running T-scores too often will either frustrate you as they move slowly, or you will be tempted to make a two into a three just for progress. Stay the course.

Chapter 23: What Could Possibly Go Wrong?

"First, they ignore you, then they laugh at you, then they fight you, then you win."

Mahatma Gandhi

For this chapter, we will lower our Positivity score to 0.5 and examine all the things that could go wrong with your journey to full Trusted Advisor status. This is your opportunity to learn from the mistakes of others and to avoid some of the pitfalls affecting other programs. Sometimes it does pay to take on a cynical yet realistic worldview as part of the planning. One facilitation trick I learned from an old hand was to ask at the start of a potentially contentious meeting, *"what are some of the things that could happen that would render this meeting useless?"* Collecting ideas and writing them down often helped to prevent or at least minimize those negatives – at least as far as general behaviour and process issues.

Six Common Mistakes, Errors, and General Screw-Ups You Should Avoid.

These can all happen even if you have followed all the advice in this book and other sources, used excellent common sense and set out a fantastic project plan with executive support.

1. No Early Successes

We need gratification, and we need to show people that we are succeeding. Even small victories count, such as setting a meeting with a difficult client or having a customer agree to be a reference for the first time. Imagine running a PR campaign for your Trusted Advisorship (it's not very "S," but there is a greater good at the end of it!), so you need to celebrate your wins and make sure that others around you are aware of them as well.

No matter how committed you may be to the program if nothing happens after 3-4 months, doubts can start to arise, and you can lose momentum. For that reason, keep a log or a journal of all your activities. Then, when something positive happens in one of your accounts or with an internal relationship, you can see the cause and effect and celebrate just a little. That is a high P for the program.

CASE STUDY: PUTTING ON THE RITZ

One of the few advantages of business travel is the ability to rack up copious airline and hotel points. My hotel chain of choice for many years has been Marriott. I periodically use my Marriott Bonvoy Points, so my wife and I can enjoy stays at the more upscale Ritz-Carlton properties. After many great vacations over the years, we now 'trust' the Ritz brand to take good care of us and to provide outstanding service. However, how do they keep up the standards of good service? By celebrating small successes.

Every day, each department within the hotel gathers for about 15 minutes. Although there is some operational talk, planning, and a few management announcements, most meetings are about customer service. The manager asks associates to share a customer success story from the previous day or week – no matter how small – as a mechanism to set the tone for that day. The associates often compete to see who can tell the best (and most successful) story. That is celebrating small successes and compensating for the occasional human or computer error by contributing to the greater brand.

---

2. Going Native

Going native[39] means adopting some or all the cultural traits of the people around you – often referring to people who live in foreign countries and distant cities from their place of birth. Those traits may include language, accent, etiquette, dress, and business practices. In the case of a Trusted Advisor, it means always taking the customer's side against your own company, often with an adversarial attitude, as you now consider yourself more of a customer than an employee.

It is a difficult situation, as one of the classic definitions of a T/A is someone who always acts in the customer's best interests. That said, reality dictates that you still need to consider whose company name is on your paycheck and who provides you with your benefits, career opportunities, and development path. Suppose you are so much on the customer's side that you take a course of action that may cause legal or moral peril to your employer or even have a significant financial impact. In that case, I'd undoubtedly counsel you to take a deep breath and to talk it through with others extensively.

Should others within your company view you as "going native," your effectiveness as an advocate and advisor for your client will significantly diminish. In addition, your colleagues will not trust you as they will question your motives.

CASE STUDY: IT WILL END IN TEARS …

Early in her career, Ann was the lead Sales Engineer assigned to a large Telecommunications company in Asia. Based in Singapore and working for a small software provider to the Telco, Ann and her sales counterpart were tasked

---

[39] en.wiktionary.org › wiki › go_native for more details. It is a colonial phrase and does not always have the most positive connotations.

with converting a departmental install footprint into a much larger and profitable corporate-wide installation. After a long and arduous 15-month sales campaign featuring significant relationship selling and rapport building, they successfully negotiated a companywide pilot.

The pilot went according to plan, and Phase I of the larger rollout began. Towards the end of the rollout, the local systems administrator decided to self-upgrade the installation for reasons best known to himself. After neglecting to take a backup, he ignored multiple written and on-screen warnings and went ahead with an upgrade – wiping out the entire configuration and project management databases. There was no doubt in anyone's mind – except Ann's-that the customer was at fault. After some diagnostic effort, Ann's company determined they could restore the valuable data with about 15 person-days of coding and loaning some significant equipment. Ann told her client to ask for the work at zero cost as *"the software allowed you to kill the databases"* and coached her client through the process. Her actions caused tremendous friction between the two companies and the use of legal posturing – all spurred on by Ann. She had clearly *"gone native."*

(The customer canceled the rollout and settled the lawsuit. The software vendor lost a potentially great client, and the telco lost the potential for a competitive edge in releasing a new product. Everyone lost.)

3. Friction And Resistance From Others

The other side of your miniature PR campaign from point #1 is that there will be no shortage of people who don't believe in what you are attempting to achieve. Some will be well-meaning, *"it's a great concept, but it will never work here because of.."*. Others will be directly confrontational and tell you that *"it's slowing down my deal"* or *"you stopped me selling that additional option."* All I can tell you is that success will happen, and do not waste your breath trying to convince them otherwise. Actions speak louder than words, and the eventual successful outcome of any T/A program ultimately defeats the nay-sayers. So, again, reflecting on the Gandhi quote to start this chapter – if they begin to fight you, you are at the final stage before you "win."

4. Giving Up

Following on from the earlier point, unless you have a remarkable string of successes, there will come the moment when you are tempted to revert to the old ways. This will typically happen about 4-5 months into the program. Becoming a Trusted Advisor is a long-term game, with long periods of minimal initial progress interspersed with rare short-term victories. That is why Positivity is so important. Find a mentor and coach who can encourage you and keep you on track. If all else fails, then email me!

Once you decide to give up, it is hard to restore the program. That is because you will already have made decisions contrary to the philosophy of the T/A, and many of your factors will have started to reverse. Your credibility with others will take a hit too. Just note that although it is hard, it is not impossible to restart.

5. Being Too Aggressive

Yes. That is right, being too aggressive. Although you want to approach the program with positivity, keep a "can-do" attitude, and spread the word amongst the uninitiated – you can overdo it. Rushing out and forcing people into meetings or pushing others to follow your lead can lead to negativity from your customers and peers. People will wonder what has changed. Although that may be an opening to explain what being a Trusted Advisor means, it can also leave you open to accusations of simply taking those actions with a self-oriented goal in mind.

What is that self-oriented goal? Become a Trusted Advisor because of the success, career implications, and (yes) revenue it may bring your way. However, your intent matters more than your behavior. For example, if you come across as too "pushy" and "forceful," it can downgrade your T-score. On the other hand, it is a fine line to follow if you are a naturally outgoing, full-throttle personality. So, apply some moderation and ensure you fully have the Trust before going to Advice!

6. The Slippery Slope

A Trusted Advisor role is rarely lost by a single act of surrender but by a series of small compromises. The first time you say, *"I'll just do it this one time"* or *"I'll make an exception"* and compromise your values or T/A goals, the second occurrence is already knocking at your door. Moreover, you will again take a big hit on your Credibility.

Over thirty years ago, Lays Potato Chips (a division of PepsiCo) had an advertising campaign with a tagline of *"betcha can't eat just one."* Unfortunately, giving in to the old ways and violating your values is like that potato chip[40] temptation. It starts you down the slippery slope, and each subsequent compromise or rationalization becomes progressively easier.

In Summary

The most common and dangerous of the preceding six mistakes and pitfalls is not finding and celebrating the small successes. By focusing on what went well (in addition to correcting anything that did not), you can maintain a positive attitude, which is an antidote for the other five errors. Not everyone will be on your side, so you learn to deal with that. Customers may be skeptical – so prove your value and earn that trust and the right to supply great advice. Finally, put your "marketing" hat on – and celebrate the wins, no matter their size!

---

[40] Or potato crisp - depending on your version of spoken English.

Chapter 24: So Now You Are A Trusted Advisor Sales Engineer

Congratulations! You've worked long and hard on several relationships, modified your behavior, and probably challenged how things get done within your company. You ran the T-score and finally qualified, based on your definition, as a T/A. Your client behaves towards you as if you have that exalted position. However, what can you do with that valued T/A status? It is just one person at one client – how can it make a difference?

This is the point at which you should reflect on the utility of being a Trusted Advisor. It is a little philosophical, but is a T/A something that you can "use," or is it something that you "have"? Using the status is (deliberately and with intent) asking your client to sponsor a meeting with someone else within his company. Having the status might be when the client volunteers, on his own accord, to set that meeting up for you – or at least ask what he could do for you within his company. I view "using" as a forced behavior that will chip away at your Trust because of the increasing S factor. No one wants to feel used. I view 'having" as a more natural behavior. Philosophy is over, but think about where you want to be and what kind of relationships you want.

The Four Basic Strategies

Once you have achieved T/A status, look at four parallel courses of action. If you thought getting to this point was hard work, it is even more complicated from now on – but a lot more fun and results-driven.

1-Maintain

Defend the gains you have achieved. That means keeping the various factor scores with all your targets. To inject some additional reality, it is also very likely that by this point, you may have picked up a few different targets based on account/pipeline activity or just opportunistically because you were in the right place at the right time. Therefore, you will automatically spread effort over more accounts and people.

It requires quite a bit of effort to maintain your T/A status. It is not something you achieve and put on the shelf like a trophy. Our experience is that 4's (or a 2 for S) are a natural high, and the 5's and 1's need work. That implies regular contact with value attached. Breaking that down further means you do not just make contact for the sake of making contact. There must be a valid reason behind the connection, and remember that you must give to get something back in return.

2-Grow

You still need to grow your existing T-scores, both with clients where you have achieved T/A status and with those you have not. This step is where you must carefully watch your time and apply the law of diminishing returns. It is easier to move a C score from a 3 up to a 4 than to go from a 4 to 5. At least it should be if you got your rubric scoring correct! One of our clients compared this to a circus juggler trying to keep multiple plates spinning on a stand. You need to pay attention to every plate, especially the ones that look a little wobbly. Unlike the plate analogy, it is unlikely a relationship will crash to the ground and break – although neglect will cause a gradual time-based degradation in your relationship. Absence makes the heart grow fonder does not apply to business-based T/A relationships.

3-Expand

If you have not already given in to temptation and expanded your T/A target list, then it is time to do so. Do this opportunistically. Over the past few months, you will likely have met several candidates who would fit into this category. The guiding principle is to select people you like and would consider building an out-of-work relationship. That makes the process far more manageable. If you pick someone because you must, there is a lot of S and little P in that decision, and it will be hard work.

Consider asking your contacts who else you should meet with within their company (not just for business) and see what they say. An introduction from them to colleagues lets you slipstream some of their internal trust and gets you off to a much better start. Make sure you circle back to your initial contact and keep them informed about how things are going. If that person is one of your T/A contacts, it can be a legitimate reason to start a value-based follow-up contact – even if it is just a short informative email.

You should be looking for individuals who could eventually become Trusted Advisors in some part of your life and career. T/A in Sales Engineering is not a one-way mechanism. You will be surprised at the people you meet who may be willing to help you and eventually become a guide, mentor, or advisor to you.

CASE STUDY: THE TRUE LONG-TERM SUCCESS OF A PROOF OF CONCEPT

Thirty-five years ago, I was in the middle of a sales cycle with A.M. Best, an insurance rating company in New Jersey. At the time, I worked for Mathematica, which sold a "Fourth Generation Reporting Language" called RAMIS. We had set up a Proof Of Concept / Benchmark with A.M Best and were competing for the business with our closest rival, Information Builders (who are still in business) and their FOCUS product. Throughout the week-long benchmark, I met a gentleman named Paul Tinnirello, the I.T. Program Manager. Probably because we faced a few technical difficulties that we had to overcome together (adversity can bring people together in sales situations), we bonded. Despite the relationship, Paul was clear that the fastest product would win the business. We won the business through a combination of luck, engineering expertise back in HQ, and a great salesperson (see chapter 4). Paul and A.M. Best became one of

---

our best customers regarding product usage, innovation, and willingness to speak publicly about our partnership.

I left Mathematica in 1988 to work for a little $80m company called Oracle. You would think the story would end there – except it didn't. Paul and I stayed in touch over the next decades through an occasional breakfast or lunch as we both rose the corporate ladder. He eventually became the CIO of AM Best and retired in 2017 as their Executive Director. The point of this story came in the late 90s when Paul asked me to write some technical articles for a book/anthology he was authoring. I agreed and struggled to churn out three or four such articles for him over the next couple of years. In turn, I learnt a lot about writing, about editing and made many contacts in the publishing arena. When the time came to write the original version of Mastering Technical Sales in 2000, I had a head start, thanks to Paul. This book may never have been written if it had not been for a malfunctioning tape drive and a stubborn IBM systems programmer 30 years ago. That is the reason Paul is in the acknowledgments of this book.

4-Share

Sharing your trust comes in two formats. The first format is an extension of Sara's conversion story from the earlier chapter. Share your successes and how you have managed to get as far as you have, given the constraints and benefits, of your company. The more people you share your story with, both inside and outside the company, the more it will help your path to becoming a T/A, and you'll gather friends and supporters along the way. You will not need to convince or sell everyone in your company; you just need a few select individuals. If you do not believe that try reading Malcolm Gladwell's fantastic book – The Tipping Point[41] – to learn about the power of individuals to get a movement started.

The second format is by sharing or lending your trust to others. By implicitly or explicitly vouching for the professionalism and knowledge of a salesperson, a peer, a partner, or anyone else you introduce to your client,

---

[41] The Tipping Point, Malcolm Gladwell, 2002 – Back Bay Books

you are lending them a piece of your trust and allowing them to shine in reflected trust from you. Think of the power of referrals (I'd bet many new hires into your company are through personal referrals rather than CareerBuilder). You must be careful in using this trust, as you must be sure that the other person or company will live up to your mission of doing the right thing for the customer. Sadly, that is not always the case, and you (and the customer) may get burnt. The loan of trust most seen by an SE happens when a new salesperson comes into an account and needs your help setting up initial meetings with the customer.

In Summary

You've completed much challenging work and climbed the first Trusted Advisor Mountain. Take a moment to catch your breath, look back, and then down at the path you have travelled. You can see that you took a few unnecessary detours and rest stops along the way – but at least you got here. Now turn around. That was the first in a long chain of mountains. There is still some considerable climbing, but you have gained altitude and become accustomed to the territory, so the fun begins.

Focus on the Maintain-Grow-Expand-Share actions and balance your time across them. There are no hard and fast rules about how much time you need to spend on each activity, so that will have to come through learning and experience. Do not ignore one of the four actions for more than a couple of weeks; otherwise, there will be consequences. That's why I like the circus plate balancing analogy (and believe it or not – it's all in the wrist[42]). Once you've reached this point, it becomes progressively more manageable, so you can make it a little more about yourself in terms of being selective about who you target as a T/A candidate and also start looking for more of your own personal T/As. Aim for kind people who make you laugh, people who make you smile, and for people who make you think.

---

[42] https://www.youtube.com/watch?v=LS70x-bQRWI : Steve The Juggler Video

Chapter 25: Your Trusted Advisor Profile

W e've delivered our Trusted Advisor Sales Engineer workshops to over 10,000 participants, most of whom are actual Sales Engineers. We have account executives, business development folks, and support / consulting people attend, although they are in the minority. During the workshop or in an immediate follow-up, we ask the participants to self-identify their position/role and to assess themselves numerically in terms of trust. That yields some interesting results.

Q1: Which Is Your Strongest (Innate) Factor?

Factor	% Score	Observations
Credibility	43	"The #1 Strength of an SE"
Reliability	24	"If you don't have this, you won't survive!"
Intimacy	13	"Absolute hardest thing for me to do"
Self-Orientation	20	"We help. We don't sell."

Table 25.1 SE Self-Rated Factors. 9,882 responses as of June 2022

This data might lead you to think.

1. As expected, Credibility beats everything else. It is a core (expected and trained-for) skill of the SE.
2. Reliability is a weak second. According to the comments, it is because of the organized and structured nature of the typical SE.
3. Self-orientation is third yet does point to the characteristic of "customer first."

4. Intimacy is the weakest of the four primary factors, playing into the persona of the introverted technical nerd. I always feel that we under-rate ourselves in this area.

Q2: Which Is Your Strongest (Innate) Factor? – By Identified Gender

Sales Engineering is a heavily male-dominated profession. Women represent about 1/8 of the typical SE population. Even that ratio is radically different depending upon the type of company. For IT infrastructure "plumbing" companies (security, networking, backup/recovery etc.), the percentage of women can be 3-5%. Applications companies are up in the 20%+ area, and soft application companies (HR, Personnel Development, Legal, and CRM/Non-Profit) can push 50%. When we take the same question and subdivide it based on identified gender, we see some differences between the sexes.

Factor	% Male Score	% Female Score	Observations
Credibility	45	38	"The #1 Strength of an SE"
Reliability	26	17	"If you don't have this, you won't survive!"
Intimacy	12	20	"Absolute hardest thing for me to do"
Self-Orientation	17	25	"We help; we don't sell."

Table 25.2 Gender Differentiation[43]

What can we draw from this data?

1. The male SE is highly likely to lead with Credibility, the female SE less so, although it is still the #1 reported factor.
2. Self-Orientation and Intimacy move ahead of Reliability for women.
3. Female SEs are better at Intimacy and therefore making initial connections than men.

---

[43] We have insufficient (but not zero) non-binary responses to date to draw any statistical conclusions.

4. (Anecdotally) Female SEs in male-oriented companies/professions are far more likely to develop skip-level T/A relationships with male and female client executives.
5. (Not shown) That hardware SEs value Reliability over Credibility.

Q3: Does Age Matter In Developing A T/A Relationship?

We changed this question several times during the survey, so we cannot present direct statistically valid data. However, we did see several trends.

1. In general, we trust older people more than younger people. For example, age is more of a positive factor for hardware and services companies. Less so with social media, cloud, and cutting-edge tech companies.
2. That is mainly because of the experience factor and just more practice in Intimacy.
3. *"Never trust anyone over 30"* does not apply. Millennials are happy to trust Baby Boomers and Gen-X-ers – if they can prove the value in the relationship.
4. Baby Boomers and Gen-X will trust Millennials, mainly if they rapidly show Credibility and Reliability and bring new ideas and concepts with them.
5. There is no clear gender/age difference in Trust.

Q4: Does The Combination Or Spread Of Factors Matter?

We also looked at the data and took the top two characteristics of each SE as a combination. Someone rarely comes into a class and rates themselves equally on all factors – so we narrow it down to the top two characteristics and take Positivity out of the equation as noise.

Combination	% Score	Likely DiSC Colours	Notes
Credibility and Reliability	57	Blue and Green	The Typical SE Subject Matter Expert. Detailed and wants to share.

| Credibility and Self-Orientation | 20 | Yellow and Blue/Green | The All-Knowing Altruist. "Harvard Professor." Gently Teaches |
| Reliability and Intimacy | 11 | Green and Yellow (with a good bit of Red) | Gets Things Done through Relationships |

Table 25.3 Common Factor Combinations

Again – looking at that data:

1. SEs really rate themselves and place great value on being Experts.
2. The "Professorial" approach is a good second.
3. The first appearance of Intimacy in a combination is at #3.
4. Credibility and Intimacy were #2 rated for female SEs.

Q5: What Does The Customer Think?

Chapter 5 – The Customer Point Of View gives you a good insight into what customers want. When we reverted to many of those same customers and asked them for their rankings of the combinations, we discovered:

Rank	Combination	Notes
1	Reliability and Intimacy	They understand precisely what I need and deliver on it.
2	Credibility and Intimacy	They know their stuff and can explain why it is important to my organization and me
3	Intimacy and Self-Orientation	They are always on my side
4=	Reliability and Self-Orientation Credibility and Reliability	(C+R): Isn't that what SEs are supposed to do anyway?
6	Credibility and Self-Orientation	Need to be challenged as they are too indirect and subtle. Can be slightly condescending.

Table 25.4 What Customers Say They Want

Note that the #1 SE combination of Credibility + Reliability is ranked #4 out of 6 by the customer.

Q6: How Can We Use This Data?

Like most data, you can read different things into it depending on your perspective. From my perspective, it shows that although technical product training (Credibility) is essential, the Professional Skills around customer interactions are even more critical. Knowing how to ask the right questions, tell stories and step away from the technology is just as important as understanding the bits and the bytes of the technology.

It also tells me that if in doubt – first work on the Intimacy, then go to Credibility, Reliability, and Self-Orientation. There is much to be said for understanding the other person's motivations.

In Summary

This data represents a sample of SEs from multiple countries and cultures and may not necessarily fit you or your organization. That caveat aside, there are still many important things to learn. Rule #1 from all this is clearly to work on Intimacy and do not always lead with Credibility.

THE TRUSTED SALES ENGINEER
WORKSHEET – SELF-ASSESSMENT SURVEY

Your Name	
Title / Company	
Identified Gender	MALE FEMALE OTHER_____
Age	16-25 : 25-30 : 31-36 : 37-45 : 46-55 : 56+
Geography	Which country/geo do you cover?

Please think about your CURRENT skill set and how they relate to the four Primary Trust Factors. Rank yourself from 1-strongest to 4-weakest. No ties!!

Factor	Rank	Notes/Thoughts
Credibility		
Reliability		
Intimacy		
Self		

Bonus #1: The Trusted Advisor At Home

Although this book focuses on the Trusted Advisor Sales Engineer at work, a good deal of it applies to your life outside work. If you have a work-life balance, you will spend more time at home with your friends and family than at work with your colleagues and customers. So how can you apply some of these principles to that part of your time?

It is actually not that hard. If you think back to Chapter 1, I asked you to write down someone in your life who you considered one of your Trusted Advisors. There is about a 75% chance that person is connected to your personal rather than your professional life. So now, first list all the personal T/A's in your life. And next, those people who may consider you one of their T/A's. You should find a little symmetry and possibly a few patterns in there. For this exercise, the more names, the better – so if in doubt, list them out!

My Personal Trusted Advisors	Those Who Consider Me A Trusted Advisor

Table 26.1: The Trusted Advisor At Home List

Unlike the business world, I am not proposing that you run a T-Score on these people and put a relationship improvement plan in place. However, if you are having difficulty building a relationship with someone important in your life (whether it's transient like your child's teacher or more permanent like a neighbor or an in-law), looking at the five factors is one potential option to explore.

It is also interesting to consider why people value your advice and in which areas. For example, I have a few people who would (I hope) consider me their T/A in entrepreneurship, writing a book or an article, international travel, and general technology. A few more would seek out financial, investment, or tax advice. On the other hand, I cannot think of many friends, for example, who would explicitly ask me for personal relationship or fashion advice. That's not because my advice in those areas is bad (although it quite possibly is..), but because there are other better sources for them to speak with – like my wife.

The Five Factors

Rather than provide some generic advice, let's look at the specific advantages that the role of a Sales Engineer may give you in terms of the five factors.

Credibility. Like everyone you meet, you are an expert on something because of your job role. No matter what your company sells, it has a use to someone and makes a difference in the lives of either individuals or a corporation. Find a way to relate that to everyday life. For example, if you work for a security vendor, you should be able to assist your friends in keeping their technology and data secure. It is your decision about how deep you want to go in that direction, as it can turn you into tech support and cement your perceived personality as a geek.

However, what is the larger role of a Sales Engineer? It is to explain something complicated in simple terms so that other technical and non-technical folks can understand it. A major benefit is being an "explainer" of things to different people. Practice doing that translation and keep it short, simple, and understandable. You may also be an expert on business travel, working from home, effective conference calls, and many other areas that you might initially gloss over.

Reliability. There is no real advantage to being an SE regarding reliability, except that you are probably used to a jam-packed schedule and handling all kinds of last-minute changes and demands. However, that adaptability can help you meet the expectations of other people. In addition, depending upon your role (usually inside vs. field SE), you have some flexibility to make workday meetings or appointments or attend breakfast or early evening functions.

CASE STUDY: FOOTBALL OR SOCCER?

In the mid-90s, I travelled into Manhattan, NY, from the Princeton, NJ area. For those unfamiliar with the location, that amounted to a two-hour door-to-door daily commute. At the time, I was also one of the coaches of a girl's travel football (soccer) team. We had practice sessions at either 6:00 or 6:30 pm on Tuesdays and Thursdays, which meant I had to leave New York City two hours earlier. Fortunately, the soccer fields were on the way to the train station, so I did catch a logistical break. No matter what happened, I did my best to make every practice session we held. Not only did I feel I owed that to the parents and the girls themselves, but it was a pleasant break from dealing with pushy Wall Street customers and the salespeople who dealt with them.

Whilst I certainly did not make every practice, I refused to miss training because someone called a random meeting or felt I needed to be in the office. Although there were two other coaches who could efficiently run the practices, I was the lead skills coach (English background!) and wanted to honour my commitment to the team.

To be fair and balanced – although I made many practices, I also took great pains to point out the length of my commute and ensured everyone knew about it. Therefore, my "S" wasn't as good as it could have been.

Intimacy. As mentioned many times, this is usually the weakest area for an SE. Your personal life is also the best area to practice this skill. Think about how many total strangers you will likely meet in the grocery store, coffee shop, or sports field. This is multiplied tenfold If you have children or grandchildren. Take the opportunity to practice conversations and initial interactions and experiment. As always, asking non-intrusive questions of the other person is the way to go. (That is difficult for an Englishman trained to either keep quiet or make some comment about the weather. Yet if I could learn it, so can you!)

With people you are a little closer to, try sharing some experiences around your week, your travels, or your customers that might be interesting or relevant to them. The role of an SE is a mystery to 99.5% of the world's population. So simply explaining what you do (see Credibility and the "explainer") and sharing something about that can go a long way. If you do manage to come up with a short and practical explanation, please email it to me, as I've been struggling with that particular topic for 25 years.

Self-Orientation. As an SE, you have skills and experiences that many people do not. The schizophrenic nature of the position, being technical + business + personable, gives you an advantage in that you can help many others out with problem-solving and general advice. Let *"how can I help you"* become your personal mantra and own the phrase. You'd be surprised at the ways these skills can manifest themselves.

CASE STUDY: THE BIBLE AND TALENTS

"I had been a member of the same church for fifteen years, and although I participated in a few committees and stewardship events, I never really found my place or role. I had no voice, could not play a musical instrument, didn't have much religious insight, and failed at teaching the 10-year-olds in Sunday School.

One Sunday morning, I sat quietly in the pew with my wife. A friend approached coughing and spluttering and asked me to read an announcement at the start of the service. He was supposed to do it but was having some allergic attack. I had no opportunity to decline before he ran off politely, and the service started, leaving me holding a piece of paper in my hand. I stood up, went to the front of the church, put on my best demo presentation voice, and made the

---

announcement. Everyone listened. Whether you believe in divine intervention or not, I had found my new role on Sundays – I was **The Announcer**."

George, Kansas City.

Positivity. There is even more room for positivity in our personal lives than in our business lives. A genuinely positive attitude makes you stand out in most cultures and countries. You have a great job, working for (hopefully) a fantastic company and/or a wonderful boss – why shouldn't you be happy? It can be as simple as:

"Hi, John. How are you today?"

"Absolutely fantastic. Thanks for asking Steve – how about you?"

Try it!

In Summary

There is much about the professional role of the SE that lends itself to Trusted Advisorship in your personal life. That happens by moving your professional skills into the personal side of things. We work in a unique role, which creates an opportunity to generate some curiosity and start working on the Intimacy and Self-Orientation factors and moving the Credibility upwards.

However, I have to conclude the chapter with the sad fact that *"I'm A Sales Engineer"* is unlikely ever to become the #1 pickup line in a bar or a conversation starter at a cocktail party.

Bonus #2: Some Fun Case Studies

During our classes, we often work on a series of small Case Studies or *"What Would You Do?"* type scenarios. They focus on the ethics of doing the right thing for the customer or developing a deeper relationship. I include a couple of them in this bonus chapter as an exercise for the reader. That means I am not supplying any answers. They make an interesting discussion at a staff meeting or a small SE offsite, as the answer is not always as clear-cut as you think.

I would caution you not to make any assumptions and to ensure that you thoroughly talk through the scenario before making your verdict. Feel free to add material to the scenario if it makes it more relevant to your company or situation. At the end of each scenario, there is a small grid featuring the five Trust Factors to help you with your answer.

SCENARIO 27.1 THE OVER-ENGINEERED SOLUTION

You are sitting in a meeting with Phil (T=6), the CIO of one of your long-term customers, and his project team. Over the past few months, you have been helping them analyze issues with their IT infrastructure and working with Sara, the new salesperson on the account, to get a proposal together.

You have been on vacation (holiday) for the last ten days, and this is your first day back at work. However, you spoke to Sara last night, and based on what you know, this should be a relatively friendly review and rubber-stamp session (you have put considerable effort into this). So, after some initial chitchat with Phil about your vacation, Sara distributes the proposal.

You scan the proposal and discover that Sara has changed the configuration and, in your quick estimation, has significantly over-engineered the solution. You notice that a) the number of ports is 20% over your recommendation, b) the amount of storage proposed is almost double your recommendation, and that c) there is an optional component the customer does not need as they could easily undertake that work by themselves.

These changes amount to an extra 50,000 in the proposal (out of a 350k total). You are horrified. Then Phil turns to you and says, "*Are you OK with this? Should I sign it?*" What next?

Part 2: Now, suppose your T-Score with Phil is much lower – say a 2 or a 3?

Complete the table below to document your decision's immediate impact on the Trust Factors. Do this for Phil and Sara.

Credibility	
Reliability	
Intimacy	
Self	
Positivity	.

Table 27.1: Five Trust Factors For Scenario 27.1

SCENARIO 27.2: GIVING THE ELEVATOR PITCH THE SHAFT

You have probably all developed and practiced an "Elevator Speech." That is when you are alone in a mythical elevator with a mythical CxO of a current or potential customer. You have 60 magical seconds as the mythical elevator zips up or down imaginary floors in the make-believe high-rise to give your finely tuned pitch. The CEO then looks at you, sees your logoed shirt and visitor badge, and says, "*Tell me about your company/ tell me why we should work with you/ exactly what is it that you do?*"

Give the Elevator Pitch the shaft (British slang for throw it away!) and instead think of three different responses:

1. You are back in that mythical escalator. Answer the implied *"what can these people do for me"* question in about 2-3 sentences, and then ask a question back.

2. You are at a cocktail party and get asked the question *"what do you do"* by an important, but unknown to you, potential client.

3. You are in the company cafeteria with one of your customers (with whom you have a good relationship; say T>=7) who says, "Hey – there's our CxO; let me quickly introduce you." So he takes you over, introduces you – and says nothing else...

Credibility	
Reliability	
Intimacy	
Self	
Positivity	.

Table 27.2: Five Trust Factors For Scenario 27.2

Afterword

"The day you stop learning is the day you stop living.."

Tetsuyama-san

I share three things learned during the creation of this book.

Firstly – how difficult and complex it can be to put a vague and tenuous concept such as "The Trusted Advisor Sales Engineer" into words. I needed over 46,158 words to make an attempt.

Secondly – publishing an eBook and "Kindle-izing" is fiendishly difficult when it comes to formatting paragraphs, headings, tables, lists, and anything that is not just pure text. The paperback version is twice as complex. Any errors in format and layout are 100% mine, despite the best efforts of reviewers and editors. Please let me know if you find any such errors via the website.

Finally – being a Trusted Advisor Sales Engineer and putting a formal program in place really works. I will leave you with a quote.

"Hi, John,

Here is a great success story about our Trusted Advisor initiative. This stuff really works!! This is the first material revenue generating success from our program.

During the September workshop, we each committed to filling out those Orange T-Sheets for two major accounts and devising a means to increase our T ratings with our contacts. At the October account reviews, we used the score as another checkpoint on the probability of closing a deal in Q4. Last week during our Business Review, we discovered three interesting facts.

1. *Every account with T >=9 closed. Based on decision maker / approver / recommenders scoring.*
2. *Only two accounts with T<=5 closed.*
3. *We need to work harder on the 5-9 range.*

In addition, we had one account that just kept piling RFPs on us. We won our fair share, but no more, maybe 30% of the total possible business. So, we picked an RFP that was not in our sweet spot, declined to bid, and offered an alternative bid. We suggested an alternative way of accomplishing their requirements and then pointed them to competitors.

*Wow! We got three of their execs on the phone to query our response and ask if we really wanted their business. We gave them the T/A response and said neither side would be happy if they bought from us based on the RFP. **C** and **R** climbed dramatically, and **S** went down. Next month they offered the first bid on a project without any competition for the first time ever.*

$400,000! Just like that.

Needless to say, we're all big fans – and we'd never have had the courage to try that move without the "science" of the T/A program behind it."

Great stuff! Go forth and trust someone!

/John

About John And Mastering Technical Sales

J ohn Care serves as the Managing Director of Mastering Technical Sales LLC. The company is dedicated to serving the needs of presales engineers across the globe through a combination of skills enablement, management consulting, and keynote speeches. It is John's goal to improve the profession of the Sales Engineer in any way he can.

He founded the company based upon the highly successful book, "Mastering Technical Sales: The Sales Engineers Handbook." Described as *"the ultimate how-to manual for presales engineers and their leaders,"* the book is now integral to new hire development at many technology companies. In addition, over 35,000 students have been trained in his Professional Skills Curriculum, which through a partnership with Up2Speed Pty. has expanded into delivery throughout Asia in English, Mandarin, Cantonese, Korean, and Japanese.

During his career, John has built phenomenal sales engineering organizations at companies such as Oracle, Sybase, Business Objects, Vantive / Peoplesoft, Nortel, CA Technologies, and HP. His responsibilities have varied from an individual level up to a VP of Sales Engineering running organizations of 200 people. He has diverse experiences as both a quota-carrying salesperson and a senior IT executive/CIO listening to salesmen and SEs trying to sell him their "solutions."

In addition to Mastering Technical Sales, John has published articles in various media outlets ranging from Infoworld and CIO Magazine to the

Wall Street Journal. He is widely credited with creating the First Law Of Discovery and the original Demo Crime Files list in 1995. The updated Fourth Edition of the main book hit the streets in 2022, and he completed *"The Sales Engineering Manager's Handbook"* in early 2020. His bi-monthly newsletter, The Mastering Technical Sales Edge, has a global subscription of over 35,000 SEs.

John holds a Bachelor of Science (Engineering) in Chemical Engineering with Honours from Imperial College, London. He served on the Advisory Board of the Fox Business School of Temple University, Philadelphia as a contributor to the International and Executive MBA Program. John currently lives in Longboat Key, Florida, with his Trusted Advisor wife and various pets.

For more information, visit the Mastering Technical Sales Website.

To contact John about this book or to arrange training and speaking engagements, email him at info@masteringtechnicalsales.com

Made in the USA
Monee, IL
24 April 2023